Your Towns and Cities ir

Hove and Portslade

in the Great War

Your Towns and Cities in the Great War

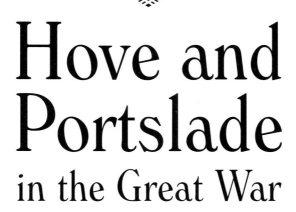

Hove and Portslade
in the Great War

Judy Middleton

Pen & Sword
MILITARY

First published in Great Britain in 2014 by
PEN & SWORD MILITARY
an imprint of
Pen and Sword Books Ltd
47 Church Street
Barnsley
South Yorkshire S70 2AS

ISBN 978 1 78303 643 1

Printed and bound in England
by CPI Group (UK) Ltd, Croydon, CR0 4YY

Typeset in Times New Roman by Chic Graphics

Pen & Sword Books Ltd incorporates the imprints of
Pen & Sword Archaeology, Atlas, Aviation, Battleground, Discovery,
Family History, History, Maritime, Military, Naval, Politics, Railways,
Select, Social History, Transport, True Crime, and Claymore Press,
Frontline Books, Leo Cooper, Praetorian Press, Remember When,
Seaforth Publishing and Wharncliffe.

For a complete list of Pen and Sword titles please contact
Pen and Sword Books Limited
47 Church Street, Barnsley, South Yorkshire, S70 2AS, England
E-mail: enquiries@pen-and-sword.co.uk
Website: www.pen-and-sword.co.uk

Contents

Acknowledgements

I would like to thank the following people; Douglas d'Enno for his introduction to publishers Pen & Sword and for the loan of two illustrations; Margaret Curson, Rare Books Librarian, Brighton & Hove Libraries, for permission to reproduce photographs from Hove Library's Great War Archive; staff at Hove Museum; N. Nic Nicol of The Prisoner of War Internment Camp Project 1914–1920 for information; Dave Sharp for his computer expertise, stories of his grandfather and relevant photographs; Norma Sharp for her eagle-eyed proof-reading; Robert Jeeves for allowing me to use two photographs from his collection; Rendel Williams for the loan of a photograph; Very Revd Dr Terry Brown for permission to use the illustration of Bishop Baddeley; various local people for sharing their memories and photographs.

CHAPTER 1

From Peace to War

In the early days of July 1914 Hove residents were drawn irresistibly towards the seafront. They flocked down there both in daylight hours and at dusk. The sight that met their eyes was indeed a once in a lifetime free show; riding serenely at anchor around 3 to 4 miles offshore was the First Battle Squadron of the British Fleet. From opposite Grand Avenue west towards the coastguard station, the ships were drawn up in two magnificent lines.

HMS *Marlborough* was the flagship and also present were HMS *Colossus*, HMS *Hercules*, HMS *Neptune*, HMS *St Vincent*, HMS *Superb*, HMS *Vanguard* and HMS *Collingwood*. The light cruiser HMS *Bellona* did not make an appearance with the rest of the ships on Wednesday 1 July, but arrived on Thursday evening.

HMS Marlborough *and other ships belonging to the First Squadron of the British Fleet paid a courtesy visit to Hove in July 1914.* (R. Jeeves)

Unfortunately, when the fleet first arrived, a light haze over the sea prevented the thousands of people lining the promenades in Brighton and Hove from seeing them clearly. The man who hastened down to the seafront to hire out his telescope at a penny a time grumbled that he was losing money. But the freelance reporter in the *Sussex Daily News* summed up the general mood:

> I saw enough to give me something of the old thrill of pride in British naval power. A huge instrument of destruction is an awe-inspiring sight, and in the hands of a bellicose nation it is terrible to contemplate. But our people, having got all the empire, they can conveniently keep in order, have come to regard the Navy as the most surest and most glorious of our defences.

Hove welcomed the sailors with open arms and Alderman E.H. Leeney, Mayor of Hove, and his councillors gave a special dinner at Hove Town Hall. They had already raised a subscription to pay for the event, which took place on Wednesday 1 July. The sailors marched through Hove and the streets were lined with cheering crowds and flag-bedecked buildings. Inside Hove Town Hall were tables adorned with floral decoration provided by Balchin & Sons while sweet peas and other plants came from St Ann's Well Gardens. Commander Usborn from

King George V and Queen Mary were crowned on 22 June 1911. Part of the celebrations included a Coronation Fleet Review held at Spithead. The British public found reassurance in the impressive size of the Fleet. (Author)

the *Colossus* was in charge of the men, who were described as a 'splendid advertisement for the empire'[1].

Commander Usborn, 'a tall, pleasant-featured officer, proved an able public speaker, and his voice rang out like a clarion'[1]. He thanked Hove for its hospitality and remarked that not every town welcomed the Navy with its exuberant sailors and guns that rattled windows and kept people awake. The dinner consisted of 'roast beef, roast veal and ham, roast haunches and ribs of Southdown lamb, pressed beef, fruit tarts, custard puddings, hot plum-puddings, cheese, butter and salad, with ale and lemonade'[1]. Besides potatoes, if other vegetables were served, the reporter did not think fit to mention them. The band of the Queen's Regiment played during the meal and when they were finished all the men were presented with packets of cigarettes and inscribed memento tobacco boxes.

The next day there was a repeat performance at Hove Town Hall for the other ranks and at the close Chief Petty Officer Webb from the *St Vincent* gave a vote of thanks on behalf of the lower deck.

Wednesday evening proved to be sultry and at 7.50 p.m. a severe storm broke out with claps of thunder so loud as to be terrifying, followed by lashings of rain. But then the weather cleared and people were anxious to see the promised event. 'Not for many years has a more enchanting spectacle been witnessed from the promenades of Brighton and Hove than was provided last night for the illumination of the First Battle Squadron. The time announced for the illumination of the eight great battleships was 9.30 p.m. and the wonder happened almost precisely to the minute, thousands of people all along the Front, on the two piers, at the windows of hotels and houses, exclaiming with delighted astonishment as the squadron suddenly revealed itself across the dark waters. The whole thing occurred with the swiftness and almost with the weird surprise of a miracle being wrought upon the sea.'[1] In fact a rocket was fired to signal the lighting-up.

There was some disappointment at the ships being anchored so far from shore, the nearest being the *St Vincent* and the *Marlborough*. Ordinary folk had hoped to be allowed to clamber aboard to see the vessels for themselves. But this delight was reserved for officials such as the Mayor of Hove and the Mayor of Brighton who travelled from the West Pier aboard the admiral's launch to pay a visit to HMS *Marlborough*. Those who could afford it could take a sightseeing trip in one of Campbell's steamers while the seriously wealthy might consider an aeroplane.

One plane trip seems somewhat bizarre and even dangerous. 'As a result of a wager, Mr Eric Pashley, the Shoreham Airport aviator, accompanied by Captain Tyrer, on a 50hp Henry Farman biplane, flew round the fleet last evening and dropped dummy bombs upon the battleships.'[2] In 1916 Eric Pashley joined the Royal Flying Corps and was based at Bertangles, near Arras. By all accounts he should have been rated as an ace of 24 Squadron, because it is said he shot down eight German aircraft as well as forcing two others down. On 17 March 1917 he was killed in a flying accident.

Admiral Sir Lewis Bayly was gratified at the welcome extended to his officers and men and he told the Mayor of Hove that he was fairly confident of paying a second visit to the town in a couple of years' time. Later on the admiral wrote a letter from HMS *Marlborough* thanking Hove for its warm welcome.

HMS *Marlborough* survived the war and in 1919 was performing her duties in the Black Sea when she was sent on an unusual and interesting mission on the orders of George V. This was to assist such members of the Russian Imperial family as had managed to avoid massacre. The group who climbed aboard the *Marlborough* included George V's aunt, the Dowager Empress Maria Feodorovna, Grand Duke Nicholas, and Prince Felix Yusupov and his wife and daughter. Prince Felix Yusupov was the ringleader in the plot to assassinate the notorious Rasputin in December 1916. But Rasputin was not an easy man to get rid of. He ate poisoned cakes without harm, was shot several times without dying, was hit about the head with an iron bar and finally in desperation the conspirators bound him and threw him into the ice-cold waters of the Neva.

Even before war was declared there was a great deal of activity at the RNVR base at Victoria Terrace, Hove. As early as 2 August 1914 all available signalmen had departed to join their ships and within three weeks most of the local division had been absorbed in the fighting forces. Eager recruits were quickly processed too. If they were judged fit, they had a week's trial at Hove Battery and were then despatched to Crystal Palace for regular training.

As soon as war was declared military authorities set about increasing their stock of horses. At Wilbury Grove, Hove, 4 August

Even before war was declared the RNVR base at Hove was the height of activity with signalmen reporting for duty. (Author)

1914 was regarded as the saddest of days in their small community. There were many fine horses in the mews where hunters, hacks or ponies were for hire or sale and carriages could be hired too. Riding lessons were given and special classes were available for children. Most of the horses were requisitioned with the standard payment being £30 per animal. Owners never set eyes on their horses again and an unaccustomed silence settled over the mews. When the mews did fill up again, the horses belonged to the cavalry stationed at Hove for a while.

An idea of the heavy toll on horses can be gauged by the experience of Captain James Vernon Lee, MC, who during the course of his military service had four horses wounded or killed under him. He was attached to the 9/Suffolk Regiment. Before the war he worked at Combridges Library in Church Road and was also an organist and musical entertainer but, unlike his horses, he survived the war.

It has been claimed that Hove held the first large recruiting meeting in the country. The event took place on 30 August 1914 at Hove Town Hall. Two large processions formed, one from Hove, the other from Portslade, coming together at Hove Town Hall. This was in answer to Kitchener's famous call to arms. It was

The proud owner of this huge charger probably chose his horse before war started. Possibly he was stationed in Brighton where this postcard was on sale. (D. Sharp)

Army authorities requisitioned horses from Wilbury Grove in 1914. (Author)

Horses were necessary for all kinds of army duties. This six-horse artillery team was sketched near the Front in 1918. (*Illustrated London News* 2 November 1918)

hoped that Rudyard Kipling and Field Marshal Lord Roberts would also attend but they were unable to do so. Hove had a particular interest in Roberts who was once a schoolboy in the town. But Sir Arthur Conan Doyle proved more than adequate. The *Sussex Daily News* reported:

> The special feature was an impassioned appeal by Sir Arthur Conan Doyle. The burning words of the famous novelist roused the audience to immense enthusiasm and will not readily be forgotten by those who heard them. Packed to excess the Great Hall could not contain all who wished to be present. It is no exaggeration to say that thousands had to remain outside, and at the close of his speech inside, the creator of Sherlock Holmes addressed the overflow without.

His speech was short and to the point delivered in a 'voice of resounding character'[3]. He said: 'You know the enemy is within sight of our shores. You know that our Army is nearly surrounded. You know there is a possibility of disaster.' He went on to say: 'You cannot live for very shame if you allow the Australians, the New Zealanders, Canadians, and best of all, those grand Indian fellow subjects

On 30 August 1914 Sir Arthur Conan Doyle delivered his eloquent rallying call for volunteers at Hove Town Hall. (Author)

Volunteers answering Kitchener's call were photographed at Brighton. Many men from Hove and Portslade had also marched in long columns to volunteer earlier in 1914. (Author)

[applause] [...] [to] come and save your own Army. I say the shame of it will never leave this country.'

He was right to be anxious because upon mobilization Britain could rely on just 733,000 men. This included the small, professional army, the Territorial Force and the Army Reserves. Compare this with Germany whose peacetime army stood at around 840,000 men but because they had had conscription for some years, on the declaration of war could conjure up 4,000,000 trained men. France also had a far larger army of 3,680,000 soldiers. It was not that the British establishment did not want conscription but that five separate Bills promoting it during the course of six years were all thrown out of Parliament. Eventually, of course, it had to happen. The message did get across and within the first five months after Kitchener's call to arms over 1,186,000 volunteers signed up for military service.

Conan Doyle himself admitted that for a long time he did not seriously believe in the German menace. But after travelling in Germany and studying General Berhardi's book *Germany and the Next War*, he became concerned enough to write an article entitled *England and the Next War* published in the summer of 1913. He was particularly worried about the submarine threat. *The Times* quoted him as saying that five-sixths of our food was shipped in from abroad, which was why he was such a strong advocate for the construction of a Channel Tunnel.

Less than two weeks after Doyle's inspiring speech, it was announced that the whole 1st Home Counties Brigade, Royal Field Artillery, Territorial Force had volunteered for active service abroad and Colonel Sir Berry Cusack-Smith was able to report to the Home Office that the brigade was 'at full strength, excellently horsed, and in a high state of efficiency'.

Conan Doyle's family was badly affected by the war. His two nephews Alec Forbes and Oscar Hornung were killed by bullets through the brain, his brother-in-law Major Oldham was killed by a sniper, another brother-in-law Malcolm Leckie of the Army Medical Service died, his brother Colonel Innes Doyle died of pneumonia after war service, and his only son from his first marriage, Kingsley Doyle, was badly wounded at the Somme and died of pneumonia too. In the Conan Doyle household there was a Miss Loder who lived with them as a member of the family. Three of her brothers were killed and a fourth wounded.

Notes

1. *Sussex Daily News*, 2 July 1914
2. *Sussex Daily News*, 3 July 1914
3. *Sussex Daily News*, 31 August 1914

CHAPTER 2

Military Hospitals

Hove was rapidly prepared for the reception and treatment of injured soldiers. Indeed the 2nd Eastern General Hospital was the first military hospital in the entire country to be mobilized. Three days after Britain had declared war, the administrative officers were already in residence.

The Brighton, Hove and Sussex Grammar School was situated on the corner of Dyke Road and Old Shoreham Road, Hove. It became a specialist unit for ear, nose and throat cases, for eye injuries, fractured limbs and for those suffering from malaria and venereal disease.

After war broke out, the Brighton, Hove and Sussex Grammar School was converted into the 2nd Eastern General Hospital. (Author)

Convalescent soldiers sitting in the sunshine at the Second Eastern General Hospital ran the risk of being inspected by curious and admiring women.
(Author)

In June 1915 a branch of the Second Eastern General Hospital was opened in the Portland Road Schools. The school authorities were only informed in March. Naturally, it caused major disruption to education as children had to go to Ellen Street Schools where a double-shift system was in operation. This meant children from both schools received a half-day of education, one set being taught in the morning and the other set in the afternoon. Then to provide variety the sets switched around. In addition, two masters from Portland Road left to join the armed forces.

One tangible advantage of the arrival of a military hospital was that the terrible state of the road surface was at last remedied. Portland Road had been notorious for its pot-holed highway with the exception of the stretch in front of the schools. The school board had been obliged to take out a loan of £3,000 to finance the cost of making up their stretch of road according to regulations when the schools were built. In April 1915 the lieutenant administrator of the hospital was so horrified at the state of the road that he requested Hove Council to undertake the necessary repairs at once. He feared the road's rough state was likely

The Military Hospital in Portland Road occupied school buildings and was opened in June 1915. (Author)

to cause increased pain to wounded men being brought by ambulance from the station.

Lieutenant Colonel Hobhouse was in charge at Portland Road for almost its whole life as a hospital since Lieutenant Colonel Reginald Jowers only held the post for its first five months. But during those early months the hospital had to deal with some of the consequences of the disastrous Gallipoli campaign, which led to hundreds of soldiers being admitted with dysentery.

At first the hospital was used as an ordinary medical and surgical establishment. There were also outdoor wards for men suffering from tuberculosis because rest and plenty of fresh air were thought to be the best treatment for the disease. Later on it became a centre for those with mental disorders or epilepsy.

As was to be expected, the ladies of Hove, headed by the mayoress, rallied around to provide the soldiers with treats and comforts to alleviate their suffering. There was even a dedicated gift room where the tide of gifts from generous private donors as well as recognized organizations, were stored.

Revd Francis Smythe, Vicar of St Barnabas for twenty years, set about raising funds so that a small chapel might be built in the grounds of the hospital. He was a warm-hearted man with down-to-earth reactions. For instance, in 1912 while taking a service at St Barnabas, a makeshift seat upon which a choirboy was sitting suddenly collapsed, sending all the choirboys into a fit of giggles. Naturally, some of the more uptight members of his flock complained about such indecorous

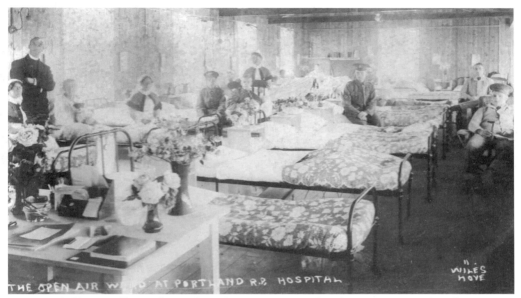

Soldiers suffering from tuberculosis were treated in the open-air ward at the Portland Road Hospital. (Author)

Convalescent soldiers from Portland Road together with their medical orderlies (wearing red cross badges) pose cheerfully for the photographer. The German helmet known as a Pickelhaube was a prized war trophy. (Author)

behaviour. But writing in his church magazine he said he would have been more worried if the choirboys had not lost their composure.

Revd Francis Smythe was also a frequent visitor to Hove Hospital, making interesting and legible comments in the visitors' book. During the Great War soldiers were treated at this institution – in fact, sometimes they outnumbered the civilian patients. In 1916, for example, there were twenty-three soldiers and only nine civilians. The more mobile soldiers proved to be an irresistible magnet for local girls who hung about the railings in Byron Street hoping for a chat. Matron was alarmed. On 7 May 1918 Smythe noted that Matron had complained about the girls who 'induce the soldiers to hang out of the windows in their night-shirts to talk to them'. Allowing that this was human nature, Smythe suggested that a word might be said to the police and perhaps a plain-clothes man could be sent up occasionally.

At the instigation of the British Red Cross Society, a number of wounded Belgians were received at Hove Hospital in the early days of

Hove Hospital treated Belgian refugees and wounded soldiers as well as civilians. Matron was alarmed when soldiers clad in their nightwear leant out of windows to talk to local girls. (Author)

the war. Afterwards, the War Office asked if some beds might be placed at its disposal and initially the committee decided that twenty-four beds for wounded British personnel would be appropriate. But in view of desperate need, this number was raised to thirty-two and finally to forty-three. The total number of military patients treated there between 11 November 1914 and 1 December 1918 came to the neat number of 888. Captain Geoffrey Bate and Lieutenant Colonel Rivaz Hunt were the medical officers in charge.

A third school in Hove was requisitioned and converted into a military hospital. It was called the East Hove (Holland Road) Hospital and occupied the buildings in Davigdor Road and Holland Road built to a high standard and opened in 1893. Indeed such was the quality of building and fixtures that there were dark mutterings from ratepayers and accusations of the school board being extravagant. Most probably they were thinking of the swimming pool, measuring 50 feet by 20 feet, constructed in the basement – a unique feature in Brighton and Hove. It was proudly claimed to be 'probably the finest in any public elementary free school in the kingdom'. When the military patients were in residence, the swimming pool was greatly appreciated.

The East Hove Military Hospital opened on 27 August 1917. It is interesting to note that several patients were already familiar with the place, having spent their schooldays there. The surgical dressing room was set up in the former chemistry laboratory while the large hall lent itself to a mess room. The convalescents could also make use of a fully equipped workshop for repairing boots or doing joinery and carpentry. The range of tools was built up over time by proceeds made from selling articles created by patients. After the hospital closed, the equipment was not wasted but dispatched to the Brighton branch of the Lord Roberts Memorial Workshops. Major Richard Whittington was the medical officer in charge for the longest time while Dr Winklereid Williams looked after special cases. Sister Winifred Ingle was in charge of the nursing staff.

Meanwhile the schoolchildren were obliged to attend Connaught Road Schools where a double-shift system was also in operation. Amongst the male staff, Walter Heather, Mr H.J. Meaton and Horace Burden were in the Sussex Yeomanry, Mr Ayling (woodwork instructor) joined the armed forces in 1915 and Mr A. Curtis joined up in 1917. Heather spent five years in the Army before returning to his teaching post at the school in 1919, but Mr Curtis did not resume teaching until 1920. Horace Burden went off to Buckingham Palace to receive his Military Medal but he could not have been a Hove resident because his name does not appear on the List of Distinctions.

The Red Cross had its own hospital at 6 Third Avenue, the house being provided by Sir Cavendish Boyle and Lady Boyle who also contributed generously to its support. It had a happy atmosphere and the soldiers liked to describe it as 'the best shop in the place'. Between September 1914 and December 1918 the number of patients treated from Britain, the empire and the USA came to 1,431.

One group of patients arrived in 1915 after having fought at the battle of Neuve Chapelle and at the famous

Lady Louise Judith Boyle was awarded an OBE for her work with the Red Cross Hospital. (Hove Library)

Hill 60. This little hill south-east of Ypres has a large military resonance. It was occupied by German troops in 1914 and the Bedfords

The Red Cross Hospital occupied large premises at 6 Third Avenue. (Author)

and West Kent regiments sought to recapture it in April 1915. British sappers were busy constructing tunnels leading from their trenches to Hill 60 where they branched out. The sappers knew full well from the sounds they heard underground that the Germans were also tunnelling and so it became a race against the clock. The British achieved their objective by a few hours and seven bombs were detonated. British troops rushed over to the German lines but it was never going to be an easy battle and at one point the German commander sent a wire to his headquarters claiming to have driven out the British. The Germans also lobbed cylinders of poison gas at the British, whose only defence was to secure wet rags around nose and mouth.

Sister Kate Jenner was the senior nurse at the Red Cross Hospital for the duration of the war. On 6 April 1918 she went to Buckingham Palace to receive her Royal Red Cross (Second class) Medal. She wrote: 'Her Majesty Queen Alexandra expressed a wish that all ladies who attended the Investiture should afterwards proceed to Marlborough House. Her Majesty presented me with a book, *The Way of the Red Cross*, and a picture with her photograph attached.'

Blinded officers under treatment at St Dunstan's, Brighton, could spend their weekends in regal surroundings at 8 King's Gardens, Hove,

These soldiers were patients at 6 Third Avenue, having been injured during fighting at Hill 60 and at Neuve Chapelle. (Author)

Blinded officers spent weekends at 8 King's Gardens, a house made famous by Edward VII's visits. (Author)

where Edward VII used to visit Mr and Mrs Arthur Sassoon. Sir Arthur Pearson owned the house and during the autumn and winter of 1917-1918 as many as forty officers stayed there. Hove Corporation allowed the men free use of Medina Swimming Baths on Sunday mornings and many residents offered hospitality.

The Countess of Chichester opened the Convalescent Police Seaside Home at Portland Road in 1893. In 1914 it was decided to place twenty-five beds at the disposal of the War Office. Preference was given to police reservists or volunteers from police forces but by 1916 it was difficult to sort the categories and it was decided that twenty beds were to be for any wounded servicemen. The men originated from all parts of Britain, from Canada, South Africa and Australia. During its time as an auxiliary Military Hospital some 544 military or naval personnel were treated. There were sixty-seven shell-shock cases besides men suffering from various wounds, malaria and trench foot. The latter affliction was not a mild skin disorder. Indeed in certain circumstances, and if left untreated, it could lead to the foot being amputated. On one occasion at the Western Front when a unit of Indian sepoys were relieved by fresh troops, they left the trenches carrying their boots, being unable to put them on because of trench foot.

Hove residents were keen to entertain convalescent soldiers.

The Convalescent Police Seaside Home did duty as an Auxiliary Military Hospital too. (Author)

The visitor's sitting room inside the Convalescent Police Seaside Home looks very comfortable. Note the splendid gramophone with horn near the window and on the right there is a harmonium. The pictures and large case with stuffed birds were probably gifts from the public. (Author)

Sometimes it was an invitation to tea at home but there were grander occasions such as the garden party at St Ann's Well Gardens on 21 July 1915 given by Bernhard Baron of 64 The Drive. There was a band to play music, tea and refreshments were served, and every soldier was presented with tobacco, cigarettes and chocolate. It was inevitable that the Indian soldiers being treated at Brighton were of especial interest to the locals and sometimes these exotic turbaned warriors were to be seen taking the air at Hove.

Indian soldiers enjoy an outing from their hospital in Brighton and their impressive vehicle is parked beside Queen Victoria's statue in Grand Avenue, designed by Thomas Brock and unveiled in 1901. (Author)

Bernhard Baron gave a garden party for wounded soldiers at St Ann's Well Gardens on 21 July 1915. He is the man standing in the centre with goatee beard, wing-collar and bowler hat. He was associated with the famous Black Cat cigarette company. (Author)

CHAPTER 3

Refugees, Prisoners of War and Shortages

On 3 August 1914 some 30,000 highly trained soldiers of the German Second Army poured across the border into Belgium. Such was their impetus that despite opposition from Belgian troops, the Germans occupied Brussels by 20 August. Until this unprovoked attack other countries had honoured Belgian neutrality ever since the Treaty of London in 1839.

There were many rumours about German atrocities in Belgium and some were fictitious. But there were genuine outrages such as the massacre at Dinant. On 22 August 1914 the retreating French Army destroyed some vital bridges, including the one at Dinant, to hold up the advancing Germans. The next day the Germans arrived and quickly set about repairing the bridge but complained that Belgian civilians were impeding progress. General von Haussen's response was to round up hostages and have them taken to the town square. That evening a firing squad executed them all, killing 612 people, the youngest being a 3-week old baby. This was the worst example of *Schreklichkeit* (frightfulness), a policy

A small brass windmill was a souvenir from happier times and it has 'Dinant' inscribed at the base. A terrible massacre took place at the Belgium town of Dinant in 1914. (Author)

pursued to subdue Belgium. In 2001 Walter Kolbow, German Secretary of State for Defence, visited Dinant and made a public apology.

People in Hove were appalled by the brutal treatment of 'brave little Belgium' and were more than ready to help Belgian refugees. On 3 September 1914 the first batch arrived at Hove and surprised the welcoming committee by turning out not to be Belgian but six Russian Jews from Antwerp. The very next day a larger contingent arrived composed of whole families. Altruism is not always easy and some of the extended families refused to be split up, which caused a headache for their hosts. But most refugees were grateful for all that was done for them

This silk card has an optimistic message, 'Gloire aux Allies'. (Author)

A silk card expressed the general sympathy people felt for 'gallant little Belgium'. (Author)

Newly built St Mary's School in Church Road, Portslade, was taken over as a Belgian hostel. Within the first six weeks 230 people, consisting of sixty-nine families, passed through its doors. Some hospitable souls offered to accommodate refugees in their own homes. This was fine as a stopgap but after a time it was felt unfair for hosts to entertain the exiles indefinitely and the Belgian Local Relief and Refugee Committee gradually assumed responsibility.

Mrs Lovett Cameron loaned 22 St Aubyns as a home for middle class Belgian refugees. The furniture was also lent, Hove Council agreed to waive the rates and taxes and even the local gas company

Newly built St Mary's Catholic School in Church Road, Portslade, was converted into a hostel for Belgian refugees. (Author)

offered to reduce its bill by one third. The committee organized free medical attention, English classes for the adults, and a school for the children. Mrs Maynard provided clothing from the depot she managed. Eventually, there were two hostels and three clubs for the refugees.

After the first wave of sympathy, it was natural for subscriptions to fall off, especially as other ravished countries such as Serbia came to public attention. But gallant Miss Ethel Grimwood, honorary secretary of the Belgian Committee, worked hard to maintain interest in the plight of the Belgians. In her report for 1917 she wrote: 'It would be a disgrace to the town if subscriptions were to fail altogether and the whole cost of our refugees were to fall on the London Committee.'

The total cost of Belgian refugee work came to £13,783 and out of this sum £6,491 was raised

Number 22 St Aubyns became a home for middle class Belgian refugees in 1914 and later on was a club for Belgian ladies. (Author)

locally. All the churches contributed in varying amounts and All Saints raised £392. Office expenses were kept to a mere £30 a year.

The house at 22 St Aubyns became a club for Belgian ladies opened by the Duchess of Norfolk. At one gathering Monsignor de Wächter, co-bishop with Cardinal Mercier of Malines, told his compatriots in December 1914: 'We refugees must show in this country that we are not unworthy of its goodness and that we merit its benevolence. We must behave so as to uphold the reputation of Belgium in a foreign land.'

For three years Father Rankin looked after the spiritual needs of refugees. He was invaluable for helping to solve many problems and also for his knowledge of French and Flemish. Unhappily Father Rankin was killed in 1917. A motor omnibus knocked him off his bicycle when he was on a pastoral visit to a Belgian family in Preston village.

Hove Town Hall became the venue for various entertainments laid on for the Belgians. In April 1915 Princess Clémentine of Belgium graced one such occasion. She made a point of walking slowly along the ranks of people, stopping to talk to them. She was then at a happy stage of her life. She was the daughter of King Leopold who refused to give permission for her to marry Prince Napoléon Victor Bonaparte even though she was aged 31 at the time of her last request. King Leopold died in 1909 and the new monarch, King Albert, gave her his

In 1918 King Albert and Queen Elisabeth of the Belgians returned in triumph to the liberated city of Bruges. (Illustrated London News 2 November 1918)

blessing. The couple married in 1910, a daughter was born in 1912 and a son followed in 1914.

At another reception at Hove Town Hall, there were 400 civilian refugees as well as some wounded Belgian soldiers who had received treatment at Hove Hospital.

The Hove ladies received the recognition of the Belgian royal house for their work with refugees and were awarded honours. La Médaille de la Reine Elisabeth was given to Miss Helen Behrends, Mrs Rosie Greening, Miss Zoé Ethel Grimwood, Mrs E.F. Maynard and Mrs Bertha Richardson.

Major John Olliver Vallance of the Royal Sussex Artillery Militia commissioned the architect Thomas Lainson to design a mansion at Hove. It was built in the 1870s and named Brooker Hall. But by the time of the Great War the family no longer lived there although it was opened up occasionally for use in fundraising events.

In 1918 some German prisoners of war arrived at Brooker Hall. The popular notion was that they were officers but they were not and they were drafted in because of a manpower shortage while officers were not required to undertake physical work under the Hague Convention. The reason behind their arrival was that Brighton & Hove Gas Company had a shortage of workers. They applied to the government for fifty or sixty prisoners of war to help shift an enormous accumulation of clinker and ashes. Under a strong, armed guard the prisoners were marched from Brooker Hall to the gasworks and back every day.

Naturally, some of the more nervous Hove residents had visions of being blown up in their beds by German sabotage. The authorities had to issue reassurances that prisoners would not be allowed anywhere near the gas-making plant. On 7 February 1918 a letter was published in the *Brighton Society* signed 'Yours faithfully, Sarcastic'. It read: 'I was glad to notice the company of German prisoners being brought into our town and was further gratified to notice that they are being housed at one of Hove's Mansion Houses.'

Local children heard about the German prisoners and peered through the railings and barbed wire at Brooker Hall for a glimpse of the notorious inhabitants. Apparently they were most disappointed to find they looked so ordinary – probably they had been reading lurid stories about the ferocious Hun and expected horns at the very least.

Brooker Hall, once the home of the Vallance family, housed German prisoners of war. (Author)

The parent camp to the one at Brooker Hall was at Eastern House, Pattishall, Northamptonshire. There were around 200 satellite camps attached to it, including Hove. The internment camps fell into two categories – working camps and agricultural depots.

While some prisoners worked at the gasworks, others were busy at local farms. In August 1917 Gladys Austen wrote in her diary about seeing a party hard at work in a field at Hove or Portslade under the scrutiny of a British soldier with fixed bayonet. Margery Batchelor (born 1903) remembered watching German prisoners working the land. They wore grey uniforms and round caps with a red band. They were chained together and there were several guards to supervise them.

According to Betty Figg, German prisoners constructed a sausage factory at Mile Oak. Later on Andrew Melville, the theatre proprietor who lived at Whychcote, used the building as a store for his theatrical props.

Albert Torrance remembered seeing German prisoners who he thought were Prussian Guards. They were marched up to his father's dental practice to have their teeth attended to. At strategic points on their grey uniforms there were circles of a different coloured material. This was so that in the event of an escape, British soldiers would have a target to aim at but the targets were so placed that such a wound would not be mortal.

In 1919 it was recorded that there had been a case of smallpox at Brooker Hall and in November 1919 the German prisoners moved out. The *Brighton Herald* (15 November 1919) had this to say:

> An interesting epoch in the war history of Hove has been ended by the disposal at auction on Tuesday and Wednesday of the fittings at Brooker Hall, used for the camp of German prisoners of war. The last of the prisoners went away a few days ago, some 100 or more, forming a motley, but happy party on Hove railway platform, looking healthy, well-fed and in regard to some at least, not devoid of that air of insolent defiance, which sits so naturally on the Germans. They have been a familiar sight on the farms in the neighbourhood and for the most part have done their work conscientiously and well. They were obviously farm hands and gave the impression of being well-satisfied with their lot. As one has observed again and again, their guarding when out at work has been of the most nominal character. At the same time, once in Brooker Hall they were looked after closely enough with sentries on duty and two circles of barbed wire.

The winter of 1916-1917 was a grim time of food shortages caused by the continuing loss of British shipping to attacks by German U-boats. At first there was a voluntary effort to convert people to the virtues of

In November 1919 the last batch of German prisoners of war waited on the platform of Hove Railway Station on the first stage of their journey home.
(Author)

economy but it soon became apparent that something more drastic was needed.

At Hove the relevant committee organized public demonstrations in Hove Town Hall in the art of bottling fruit and wartime cookery, and these were well attended. One particular meeting was a unique event because the audience was composed entirely of domestic servants. Mr Victor Milton, who was butler to Lord George Nevill at Palmeira Square, took the chair. Other special speakers were Mr Legge, butler to Mr Reuben David Sassoon of 7 Queen's Gardens, Hove, and Mrs Harvey, housekeeper to Sir Sidney Greville, Comptroller of the Household and Treasurer to the Prince of Wales, who lived at the old Hove Manor House. It was stated that 'no war meeting was more unanimous or more enthusiastic'[4].

On 2 May 1917 the food shortage situation was serious enough to warrant a Royal Proclamation in which King George V exhorted his subjects 'to practice the greatest frugality in the use of every species of grain'. He wished bread consumption to be reduced by at least one fourth. He also wanted horse owners to stop giving oats or other grain to their charges unless they had the requisite licence from the Food Controller that it was in the national interest to maintain a particular breed. The Proclamation was read out in every church and chapel throughout the land on four successive Sundays.

Food rationing began at Hove in August 1917 with the formation of the Local Food Control Committee, whose headquarters were at Kirby

This wartime poster brings home the reality of invasion fears. (From *Hove and the Great War*)

BOROUGH OF HOVE.

INVASION

Instructions to Inhabitants

(1) INHABITANTS REMAINING IN HOVE

Unless the Military Authorities otherwise order, you may remain in the Town.

Stay quietly in your houses.

(2) REMOVAL FROM HOVE.

All those persons who desire to leave the Town must carry out the following instructions:—

METHOD.   Leave on foot or by private transport. Main roads blocked :

No Railway trains available.

DIRECTION.   PROCEED NORTH-WEST, over the Downs.

Special Constables at cross roads will direct you.
Obey their instructions.
Take to fields when necessary.

WHAT TO TAKE.   Money, Food and Blanket.

House at the top of Second Avenue. Mrs Woodruff, widow of Hove's first mayor, lent the premises.

Mr J.B. Fleuret was appointed executive officer and faced a mammoth task with no precedents to guide him. But he was determined the distribution of food should be fair to rich and poor alike and, indeed, when cheese was available it was always despatched to the poorest districts first. When the committee discovered some people could afford to purchase cream at the expense of the rest of the milk, they prevailed upon the Ministry of Food to forbid the sale of cream except to genuine invalids or children.

In 1918 the two towns formed the Brighton and Hove Meat Advisory Committee, which each week purchased the required amount of meat and sold it on to individual butchers according to their number of registered customers. This prevented profiteering and ensured fairness as regards quality. It was apparently a unique enterprise in the country as a whole.

There were also attempts to persuade bakers to use a percentage of potatoes in their bread making and they were given subsidised supplies as an encouragement.

It was stated that the average population of Hove during the war years was 48,000, including visitors. But Hove's population has always been subject to fluctuation and every single move in or out of town required additional paperwork. It is interesting to note certain categories needed special consideration. There were 1,800 Orthodox Jews, 1,000 invalids and 200 vegetarians.

Food shortages led to an increased interest in allotments. Under the government's 'Cultivation of Lands Order' Hove Corporation was able to take over areas of waste ground and instead plant vegetables. Cultivation of land in Hove Park was allowed as far north as the bridle path and some of the allotments there were not relinquished until 1923. By 1920 there were between 1,300 and 1,400 allotment-holders at Hove. At St Ann's Well Gardens, flowerbeds were dug up in favour of potatoes.

Fuel was another bone of contention. Just as the war was drawing to its close, the fuel situation became so critical that in the summer of 1918 Mr H. H. Scott, Hove Borough Surveyor, was appointed fuel overseer. He was assisted in his task by a committee composed of councillors, representatives from coal dealers and coal merchants and from the gas, electricity and railway companies. The district covered West Blatchington and Preston Rural as well as Hove. 'In a seaside town like Hove the task was rendered more difficult than usual by the numerous changes of tenancy continually taking place.' Each household was allocated coal, gas and electricity according to the number of rooms in the house. It was stated that the Fuel Office had to deal with 10,426 application forms and restrictions were still in place a year after the Armistice.

Notes

4. Walbrook, H. M., *Hove and the Great War*, Hove 1920

CHAPTER 4

Women and War Work

The Great War made a huge difference to women. It was not just the absence of men-folk but a whole re-evaluation of the status of women and what they could contribute to society in general outside the confines of a home. It certainly made a difference to the thorny subject of female suffrage. Even the most die-hard traditionalist found it hard to continue denying women the right to vote after their contribution during the war. For many women, wartime work brought a sense of liberation and purpose. They undertook work that would not have seemed appropriate in peaceful times. Even ladies who had existed as ornaments in their drawing rooms found exhilaration in organizing committees or fundraising events, seeing to the needs of wounded officers or supervising the despatch of boxes full of 'comforts' for troops or prisoners of war. By July 1918 some 7,310,000 women were in paid work, but this figure does not include the thousands of female volunteers.

Walbrook neatly summed up the general amazement of men at what had happened. He wrote:

> Surely the most picturesque feature of the whole social revolution effected by the war was the woman in uniform. Thousands of women war-workers, such as bank clerks, for example, wore only their ordinary costumes, and the women patrols wore a distinguishing badge. But the post-women, the tram conductress, the taxi chauffeuse, the land girl, the milk girl, the girl who brought round the bread and the girl who called at

regular intervals to 'take the register' of the gas meter all wore a distinctive garb if not a complete uniform. So also did the workers at the depot and we recall occasions at the town hall to which they went in their hundreds wearing their snow-white overalls and caps. Add to these the thousands of Wrens, WAACS and Voluntary Aid Detachment workers [...] all of whom went about in full uniform, and some idea will be conveyed of the sartorial metamorphosis of the sex in those amazing years.

In 1918, out of a total of eighty-seven bus conductors licensed to operate in Brighton and Hove, no less than eighty-one were women. They needed to be good at mental arithmetic to be able to give the correct change quickly. One letter-writer thought there should be fewer buses running on Sundays to give the young girls a break from their hard work. Later on in 1918 there came a time when there were no buses or trams running at all because the drivers and conductors had come out on strike over the matter of an equal bonus. People were left stranded at bus stops all over town with no idea of what was going on. The strike lasted from Monday afternoon on 19 August to Wednesday midnight on 21 August, when it was called off. Apart from the inconvenience caused to the general public, the one advantage of the strike was being able to breathe the summer air without the fumes of petrol or benzine assaulting the nostrils.

The trams employed women conductors as well. The young lady in the photograph called Kitty (surname unknown) was a good friend of Mabel Sharp of Portslade. Kitty is wearing the uniform of Brighton Corporation Tramways, as identified by the small cap badge. Underneath that there is a brass badge with the word 'Conductor'.

In 1915 Southdown Motor Services began to employ women as typists and clerks. Up to that stage letters had been hand-written by men but women used typewriters. Their employers were gratified to find them more professional. They were also, of course, cheaper to hire than men.

Kitty was a friend of Mabel Sharp (neé Perrin) and she was pictured wearing the uniform of a Brighton Tramways conductor. (D. Sharp)

In around 1917 Marie Mitchell proudly wears her uniform as a Southdown bus conductor. (E. Masters)

Women started out at a modest rate of pay of two shillings and sixpence a week, but with experience they could graduate to all of six shillings a week.

Southdown Motor Services employed female conductors too. One such was Marie Mitchell who was born in Adur Terrace, Southwick, right next door to the birthplace of the celebrated contralto Dame Clara Butt. Later on Marie's family came to live at 15 St Nicholas Road, Portslade. Girls had to be aged 18 before they could become a conductor and Marie was only 16 when she applied, so she had to stretch the truth. But she was proud of her job and her uniform, and lost no time in visiting the studio of H.W. Tubbs, the well-known Portslade photographer. As can be seen, her skirt reveals a pair of highly polished boots. Normally, boots would not have been so visible but Marie shortened her skirt because she thought the standard issue too long. The authorities were not amused and she was almost dismissed because of it.

Towards the end of the war driving conditions deteriorated. Lights on vehicles were dimmed due to bombing fears while essential repairs to roads were not carried out. It was claimed that the worst stretch of road in Sussex was the seafront road between Hove Street and the Halfway House pub in Station Road, Portslade. Some potholes were 8 inches deep or more.

It was on the buses that Marie Mitchell met her future husband George Masters. He had spent three years of the Great War with the Army Service Corps, Sussex Yeomanry, and had learned to drive motor vehicles. He was invalided out of the Army after contracting rheumatic fever. When sufficiently recovered, he took a job with Southdown driving motorbuses. The couple lived with Marie's parents at first and they went on to have three children.

Amy Broomfield, Land Girl, stands perched above the small wheel of a wagon near the Stonery, Portslade. (Hove Library)

The twins Albert and Amy Broomfield were born in 1898. Their father John Broomfield farmed extensively in Mile Oak, Portslade. Amy was always something of a free spirit and possessed a volatile temper. Her three brothers and the farm workers learned to read the weather signs by looking at her face. She was tailor-made to be a Land Girl in the Great War and continued to work her father's land as well as enjoying the company of other Land Girls.

John Broomfield expected his three sons to remain at home and help with the farming even if they would have preferred a different occupation. Amy's twin Albert was desperate to go to sea but instead remained dutifully at home, passing on his love of the sea to his son. Maurice made a bolt for freedom in 1916 by enlisting under age. But when his mother informed his Commanding Officer of his true age, he was soon sent home. Only Frank managed to serve in the Great War but he came back to Portslade a changed man and died of his injuries in 1920.

Portslade Gasworks was constructed in the 1870s, with various enlargements over the years. By 1914 it was producing 1,500 million cubic feet of gas a year. The gasworks did their bit for the war effort by producing bombs for the Stokes trench mortar (F.W.S. Stokes invented the Stokes Mortar in 1915; it was a rapid-firing weapon but had a pronounced recoil) and benzol, which was used in the manufacture of high explosives. But the place was labour-intensive and

Portslade Gasworks had a chronic shortage of workers during the war and had to employ women, pensioners and German prisoners of war. (Author)

the management was hit when so many young male employees of military age went off to serve in the armed forces. The company was obliged to employ 150 women and boys plus a few pensioners.

Although the work was tough and physical, the women expected no favours and were hard workers. They wore bulky overalls and after work trudged home wearily with their skin an unhealthy shade of yellow caused by sulphur fumes. Town gas was more toxic compared to North Sea gas and fumes sometimes overcame the workers. The remedy was to drink a glass of milk to absorb the poison.

Some of the women assisted in moving the coal from dockside to works. The colliers at that time were relatively small with an average of 800 tons of coal in the hold. But there were no mechanical helps in unloading. When the wagons were full, the women pushed them along a designated tram road and thence to the retorts. Fred Lucas was the gasworks' ferryman and he married one of the women who worked there. His wife was always very proud that on her marriage certificate under the heading 'occupation' was 'gas labourer'.

Ethel Chandler was not born in Portslade but came to live there in 1912 and remained for the rest of her life. Even in her 90s, you could discern her Suffolk accent. Her aunt was instrumental in moving the Chandler family from Suffolk because she found a good house at 79 Trafalgar Road, Portslade for a rent of ten shillings a week. The family consisted of the widowed mother, 17-year-old Ethel, sister Hilda and brother Horace. Her aunt worked as a cook/housekeeper for an old lady in Hove and she heard of a place going for a parlour-maid, just right for Ethel.

By the time the Great War broke out, the old lady had died and Ethel was working as a cook's assistant in Portland Road. Life changed when she saw a recruiting poster for women to join the Army in the *News of the World*. The idea was that women would undertake administrative work as clerks, signallers and telephonists as well as more practical tasks like cooking or being dispatch riders, thus releasing men for active war duty. The campaign was so successful that by 1918 some 57,000 women had fulfilled various roles in the Army.

On 2 December 1916 Ethel enrolled in the Women's Legion, which the Marchioness of Londonderry founded in July 1915. There were many different organizations that a woman might join but most of them were voluntary and presumed the volunteer had sufficient

Ethel Chandler served in the Women's Legion. In this photograph she is standing on the left with her sister Hilda in front of their home at 79 Trafalgar Road, Portslade. (E. Chandler)

funds to buy her own uniform. The Women's Legion was different because it offered women paid work and provided a uniform and was therefore attractive to the working classes. In January 1917 the Women's Legion was renamed the Women's Auxiliary Army Corps. Although the women wore a khaki uniform there was no question of them being on an equal footing with men. There were no commissions and they were not subject to the same military discipline. The hem of the regulation army skirt was not permitted to be more than 12 inches above the ground and the usual headgear was a neat close-fitting khaki cap, but Ethel's headgear was a pudding-bowl type hat with a broad rim.

Life as a cook in the Army was busy but there was a great sense of camaraderie. Reveille was at 6 a.m. but as the cooks had to be down at the cookhouse by that time, it meant an even earlier start. At least the men kept the fires well-stoked for the women cooked on freestanding coal-fired ranges, frying bacon and eggs in deep ration tins. Large boilers for heating up water were always on the go to replenish the huge tea urns. Ethel and her companions cooked for around 200 men, members of the Machine Gun Corps and later the Tank Corps.

Some of the more energetic women enjoyed a social life in the evenings with the occasional whist drive. But often Ethel was content to retire to her cubicle for an early night. On some nights a military band giving soldiers a musical send-off as they marched away to war disturbed their slumbers. Then came the sound of sobbing as girls wept for their departing sweethearts. Ethel came home from the Army in December 1919. She never married because she said that nobody could ever replace the sweetheart who failed to return from the war and she always kept a framed photograph of him near at hand. For her the Great War cast a long shadow.

Women began to undertake work they had never done before. At Hove Mr F. Cawardine of Mortimer Road was one of the first local employers to take on women to do carpentry work. Although technically the work came under the heading of munitions, they did not work with explosives but made suitable boxes to contain ammunition and shells. After a government appeal in the spring of 1917, many Hove women left for London and other places to work in large shell-filling factories, often under dangerous conditions. These women earned the unfortunate nickname of 'canaries' because exposure to explosives turned their skin yellow with even their toenails being affected. After work when they had a good wash the water looked bloodstained. But women viewed such work as a valued alternative to the humiliation of domestic service and, besides, the pay was better.

At the other end of the spectrum were Sir George and Lady Casson Walker who had enjoyed an enviable lifestyle in India during the high days of the British Raj. Sir George was a member of the Indian Civil Service from 1875 to 1911. He became financial minister to the Nizam of Hyderabad (1869-1911), who was the richest prince in India and entitled to a twenty-one-gun salute. The sixth Nizam with whom Sir George worked was known as Mahboob (the beloved) Ali Pasha. He was modern enough in outlook to sanction the setting-up of a school to educate girls who lived in Purdah (this was the custom whereby women occupied separate quarters, secluded from the eyes of men) on the condition that Lady Casson Walker was president of the ladies committee. The school was established in 1907 with four girls and called originally the New Zenana School but eventually it acquired the name of Mahbubia after the Nizam. It still flourishes today, albeit now open to girls of all creeds.

In 1910 Lady Casson Walker was decorated with the Kaiser-i-Hind medal and Sir George was a Knight Commander, Order of the Star of India. But with the advent of a new Nizam of Hyderabad in 1911, Sir George and Lady Casson Walker retired to Hove where so many ex-India hands congregated. During the Great War she put her organizational skills to good use by supervising the running of the Municipal Kitchen during the first year of its operation. It was stated that Lady Casson Walker's 'guiding hand was visible in the smooth and pleasant working of the whole institution'.

The Municipal Kitchen opened in September 1917 at Livingstone Road. Hove already had a tradition of providing soup kitchens at times of economic stress but the Municipal Kitchen provided more than just soup. Forty customers could sit down upstairs and enjoy their meal whereas with the soup kitchen people used to carry soup home in a receptacle such as the ubiquitous enamel jug or even the china/pottery washstand jug. The dining room was converted from an erstwhile rifle saloon and was much patronized by the girls of the neighbourhood who worked in the laundry or a factory. But everybody was welcome, regardless of class or gender. The menu on the first day of opening was as follows:

Lentil soup	2d
Stewed mutton and peas	4d
Cold roast beef	6d
Blancmange and fruit	2d
Jam roll	2d
Baked potatoes	1d

The Municipal Kitchen did not close until spring 1919 and the diligent committee was able to return to Hove Council all the money that had been advanced to pay for the equipment. Sir George died at Hove in April 1925 at the age of 70 and his widow moved to Ireland to live with Jennie, one of the couple's two daughters.

Lord George Montacute Nevill was the third son of the First Marquess of Abergavenny. In 1882 he married 18-year-old Florence Mary, only child of Mr Temple Soanes of Pembury Grange. The couple lived at Palmeira Square, first at number 14 and later at number 22. Lady George was part of the fashionable throng and the Press used to comment on the clothes she wore at the famous Sunday morning church parade on Brunswick Lawns. For example, in September 1910 the *Brighton Gazette* commented that she looked 'very chic in a coat and skirt of pale heliotrope and large Merry Widow hat'.

But during the Great War she had more pressing matters on her mind, especially with one of her sons in uniform. On a visit to a hospital in London the number of nerve-affected soldiers captured her attention. She thought they looked out of place in an ordinary hospital and would stand a better chance of recovery in a specialist hospital. She set about raising funds for such an enterprise. She persuaded her husband to act as honorary treasurer and Mr D'Avigdor Goldsmid kindly lent her the house at 24 Palmeira Square. The Lady George Nevill Hospital opened on 17 March 1917 as the neurological section of the Second Eastern General Hospital. It possessed the latest electrical equipment including 'radiant heat and light baths, X-rays and high frequency applications'. Mrs Searle, the matron, headed a staff of devoted nurses. They found great satisfaction in their work because men who might have otherwise

The houses pictured here are 22, 23 and 24 Palmeira Square. Lord George Nevill, his wife and family lived at number 22 and the Lady George Nevill Hospital was at number 24. (Author)

Lady Nevill was also responsible for providing the first fleet of ambulances at Hove. The photograph shows the St John's Ambulance Brigade and Red Cross motor ambulances of Brighton and Hove 1918-1919. (R. Williams)

been labelled as incurables were, with kindness and treatment, restored to some semblance of normality. The hospital did not close until May 1919 and the equipment was presented to the Royal Sussex County Hospital.

Lady George also provided the first local fleet of ambulances run jointly by the Red Cross and the St John's Ambulance Brigade. She was deputy president of the Brighton, Preston and Patcham Division of the Red Cross Society. For recreation she enjoyed a game of golf and was president of the Brighton and Hove Ladies Golf Club. She was fond of animals and in 1915 donated a drinking trough for horses placed opposite St John's Church. She was also president of the Brighton section of the National Canine Defence League.

Lady George was not the only family member interested in the welfare of injured soldiers as her daughter-in-law, Mrs Guy Nevill, had embarked on a similar course. Mrs Guy Nevill's father, Mr J.W. Larnach, undertook the entire cost of equipping and maintaining a hospital set up in a house on Hove sea-front, lent by Mr D'Avigdor Goldsmid. There was an operating theatre and a fully trained staff. The establishment was called the Larnach Hospital for Wounded Officers and opened in June 1916 with Mrs Guy Nevill as superintendent.

After the war Lady George Nevill's work was recognized and she was created a Commander of the Order of the British Empire and became a Lady of Grace of the Order of St John of Jerusalem.

But the war also brought heartache when her younger son, 34-year-old Eton-educated Captain Rupert William Nevill of the 15/Rifle Brigade, died at home in 22 Palmeira Square on 3 November 1918. He had been invalided out of the Army ten months before his death and was probably already in a weakened state when he became one of the many who suffered from the virulent illness known as the Spanish flu followed by pneumonia. He had retired from the Army before hostilities with the rank of major, but when war broke out he rejoined his old brigade with the rank of captain. In healthier times he had been a keen member of the Eridge Hunt.

Lady Florence Mary Nevill was awarded the OBE for her work with the hospital she founded and her work with the Red Cross. (Hove Library)

In 1920 Lord George Nevill died. His widow received messages of condolence from Queen Mary and Princess Louise, Duchess of Argyll. Lady George died in 1929 and both she and her husband are buried in Hove Cemetery near the chapels. But their son Captain Rupert Nevill lies buried in the churchyard of Holy Trinity, Eridge Green, which is close to Eridge Castle, the family seat of the Marquess of Abergavenny.

Mrs Barney Barnato, the widow of the famous millionaire who made his fortune in South African diamonds, also established a hospital at 38 Adelaide Crescent, Hove, for wounded soldiers called Hove Military Hospital. It could take twenty patients at a time. Mrs Barney Barnato lived not far away at 4 Adelaide Mansions.

The Hove Depot opened on 6 April 1915, the third in the kingdom, the other two being at Ipswich and Kensington. Indeed it was a conversation with Mrs Cobbold of Ipswich during which she described the sort of work done at their depot that inspired Mrs Bromley Davenport to undertake a similar task at Hove. Mrs Davenport together with three other ladies, lost no time in calling upon Alderman and Mrs Sargeant, Mayor and Mayoress of Hove, to outline their ideas. There was an enthusiastic response and within a short space of time the depot was in existence.

At first the depot occupied two modest rooms at 4 Grand Avenue but eventually it took over the whole residence, said to be one of the largest private houses in Brighton and Hove, and into Airlie House opposite. From the time it opened until the depot closed in March 1919, the remarkable number of 3,000 voluntary workers, nearly all of them women, toiled away diligently. The women came from all levels of society and for hygiene purposes, since they were making medical necessities, all wore a white nurse's uniform. Moreover, each person paid sixpence a week for the privilege of working there for free. This money was spent on administration, which meant every penny received in donations was expended on purchasing raw materials. The total cost of the work undertaken during those years came to £29,000 and nearly all of it was raised at Hove through donations, bazaars, flag days, rummage sales and church collections.

Many different articles were created, from swabs, dressings, bandages, ward linen, splints and crutches to dressing gowns, slippers, socks, mufflers and mittens. The papier mâché workers, metal workers and carpenters occupied Airlie House. Miss Dorothy Roberts was the

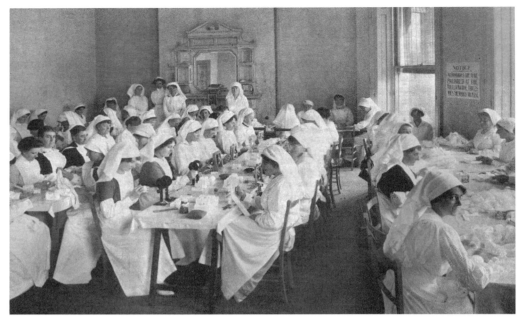

Many volunteers worked at Hove War Hospital Supply Depot. The elegant mirror in the background is a reminder of the fine house that 4 Grand Avenue once was. A block of flats now covers the site. (From *Hove and the Great War*)

honorary surgical superintendent during the first year and it was her technical knowledge that led to the success of the surgical work. It was while Lady Elsie Shiffner was busily engaged at the depot that she was invited to direct a new department in the Indian Hospital at the Royal Pavilion entitled the Provisional Limbs Department but popularly known as Lady Shiffner's Room. In this space Dr Martin's plaster stump-buckets were made under her supervision. (Stump-buckets were used to create a plaster of Paris mould to protect the stumps of amputees.)

For seven months the depot was privately run but in November 1915 the Army Council stepped in to co-ordinate voluntary work throughout the entire country and this led to greater efficiency and less duplication. Branches of the Hove Depot were set up in various parts of Sussex and there were even a couple over the border in Surrey and one in Kent. Locally, there were branches at Portslade, Shoreham, Worthing and Rottingdean. There were also affiliated groups of workers formed mostly by church groups and schools. These branches and offshoots maintained financial independence but sent their work to the central Hove Depot on a regular basis.

The extraordinary amount of work produced from 6 April 1915 to 21 March 1919 can be seen below:

Roller bandages	780,974
Sewn bandages	154,780
Splints (metal/wood)	13,164
Crutches, bed-cradles, bed rests & tables	6,353
Dressings & appliances	884,026
Ward linen, etc	80,413
Articles of clothing, etc	102,054
Slippers and 'trench feet'	16,629
Socks, mufflers, mittens, etc	37,221
Miscellaneous	31,062
	2,106,676

One of the ladies working at the Hove Depot had a son serving abroad with the Royal Army Military Corps who wrote the following letter:

At 4 pm the Germans shelled on our position very heavily and I was dressing a number of wounded in our front line. One man had a badly fractured arm and I had no suitable splint and should have had to improvise a very rough one. Just then a man ran up and gave me a paper parcel containing two beautiful waterproof-covered angular splints, which just met the case. The paper was labelled 'War Hospital Supply Depot, Hove, Sussex.' Wasn't that curious?

From a casualty-clearing station in France in September 1916 came this letter:

Of all the various things we receive yours are the very best. They were so beautifully made and finished and every little detail thought of.

Those at sea also had cause to be grateful to the Hove Depot. From an unnamed trawler the following letter was sent:

I have the honour to thank you on behalf of the men for the socks, mittens, helmets, mufflers and cardigans you have so kindly sent us. I can assure you that these gifts are much appreciated and will keep the men warm during the cold weather.

Hove also became responsible for supplying medical comforts to British prisoners of war. In 1916 the work started off in one room at 4 Grand Avenue but soon needed larger premises and went first to 19 Second Avenue and then to a house in Third Avenue. The Prisoners' Comfort Fund was founded after news of the terrible conditions at Wittenberg Camp, when German doctors deserted their post during an epidemic of typhus. Consignments were sent to the principal camps in Germany, Austria, Turkey and Bulgaria. After the Cambrai campaign in November 1917, British prisoners were desperate for clothing and within three days the Hove Fund had dispatched 12,000 articles.

Sergeant C. Lowman of the Hampshire Regiment wrote in February 1919:

I have recently returned from Turkey where I have been a prisoner for the past three years. I was captured at Kut with General Townshend. Owing to the hardships we endured in the

There was constant activity in the packing room of the Invalid Comforts Fund for prisoners of war. Packages were sent to the main camps in Germany, Austria, Turkey and Bulgaria. (From *Hove and the Great War*)

For a while the Prisoners' Comforts Fund worked from this house at 19 Second Avenue. (Author)

siege and the terrible way we were treated after falling into the hands of the Turks my constitution was completely wrecked. I now feel it is my duty to write and thank you for your kindness in sending us parcels of medical comforts, which I am sure saved the lives of many prisoners in Turkey.

Mrs Muriel Bromley Davenport, who founded the depot, was created a Commander of the Order of the British Empire for her work. Her husband Captain Hugh Richard Bromley Davenport was educated at Eton and Cambridge and was a member of the Stock Exchange. He was born in 1870 and although not a young man, he did his bit too by enlisting in June 1917. He taught physical exercise and bayonet training to the British Expeditionary Force in France. Afterwards he was awarded the OBE (Military Division). The couple lived at 6 Medina Terrace.

Lady Elsie Shiffner was also awarded the OBE. But there was some debate about whether or not she should be included in the Distinctions part of Hove's War Record as a Hove resident. Lady Shiffner was more

Mrs Winifred Field of North Road, Portslade treasured these soldier postcards – if only we knew their identities. Whoever he was, he looks like a man accustomed to issuing orders. (Author)

Two copies exist of this 1916 portrait of Joe (no surname unfortunately). One was sent from France to his brother George, 'wishing you all the best of luck old boy', and the other dated 31.10.16 was inscribed 'with love to Mother and all at home'. (Author)

A copy of this portrait, taken in 1918, was sent to his sister Rose from Arthur (the standing soldier) on duty with the British Expeditionary Force. On the back Arthur has written, 'This is a photo of the sanitary squad', but was it a joke or a fact? Arthur also wrote, 'How do you like my "posh" watch chain?' (Author)

than willing to answer Mr Lister's questions and wrote him a letter detailing how she lived at 3 Queen's Court, Hove from 1912 to 1914, then moved to Lewes, returning to Hove in February 1917 to live at 57 Brunswick Square where she remained until December 1919.

Mrs Isabella Emma Sandeman received an OBE too for her work with the local branch of the Red Cross, being deputy president, and her war work, which included stints at the Hove Depot with the making of papier mâché splints and also undertaking searches for wounded and missing personnel. She lived at 14 Second Avenue with her husband Captain William Wellington Sandeman, who retired in 1888 after twenty years of service with the 2nd Seaforth Highlanders and held the Afghan Medal. But despite his age, he also played his part in the Great War as commander of the 4th Royal Sussex Volunteers from 1915 to 1919 and received an MBE.

Their son, Second Lieutenant William Alastair Fraser Sandeman, was born at Hove on 29 March 1889, educated at Harrow and Sandhurst, and enlisted in the Gordon Highlanders in August 1909. On 13 October 1914 near Bethune he was badly wounded and his regiment was obliged to leave him behind when ordered to retire. He became a prisoner of war and died in hospital at Laventie on 19 October 1914. It is interesting to note that in St Andrew's Old Church, Hove, there is a plaque to the memory of Lieutenant Henry Sandeman, resident engineer and private secretary to the governor of the island of St Lucia, who died of yellow fever in 1852.

Mrs Field also kept the fragile silk postcards reproduced in this book. No doubt these unknown soldiers sent them home from the Front. This one is 'to my dear sister' with a red rose. On the back 'With best love to Kitty' is written in pencil. (Author)

CHAPTER 5

Portslade

David Sharp lived at 81 Trafalgar Road, Portslade for thirty-seven years but he travelled a long road before settling down here. He was born in 1897 in Kelvinside, Glasgow, in a typical tenement. His parents must have found their life a struggle because, like many other Scots before them, they dreamed of making new lives for themselves in Canada. In 1911 Sharp's parents discussed their plans and there was the exciting possibility of travelling aboard the *Titanic,* which was due to make her maiden voyage in 1912. But they decided the expense was too great because of the cost of train fares to Southampton. Instead they took the cheaper and more immediate option, and as it turned out the safer one, of sailing to Canada from Liverpool in 1911. The family consisted of David Sharp, his mother and father, sister and brother.

They settled in Winnipeg but three years after their arrival war broke out in Europe. David Sharp was desperate to do his bit but he was too young to enlist because in Canada you needed to be 19 years old. Many people, including influential ones, expected the war to be of short duration with many saying it would all be over by Christmas.

Sharp solved his dilemma by claiming he was over 19 when he enlisted on 1 January 1915. His appearance might have had something to do with it because he was 5 feet 11 inches, quite tall for those days. There is a marvellous photograph of him taken in Winnipeg resplendent in the full Highland rig of the Queen's Own Cameron Highlanders. He is carrying a bugle and he also played drums in the band. You needed to be of Scottish descent and of good character to be able to join. This regiment was a feeder for the 44th Battalion Canadian Overseas

Expeditionary Force, but after training Sharp was assigned to the 32nd Battalion Canadian Infantry.

On 1 June 1915 he sailed from Montreal aboard SS *Grampian.* However, shortly after his arrival in England he was struck down by pneumonia and was sent to hospital where he was placed in a bed by a window. Whether it was due to the severity of his illness or whether it was because of strong sunlight playing on one side of his face, his eyesight was badly affected. In fact he was semi-blind for a while and in no shape to fire a rifle. He was given an Honourable Discharge and sailed back to Canada to complete his formal discharge papers in Quebec in July 1915.

His family must have been pleased to see him back safely but he was so disappointed that as soon as he had fully recovered, he was off to enlist again and apparently he was passed as fit for service. This time he was assigned to the 45th Battalion. He sailed aboard SS *Lapland* and arrived in England in March 1916.

David Sharp was photographed in 1915 in Winnipeg, Canada, wearing the uniform of the Queen's Own Cameron Highlanders. (D. Sharp)

Perhaps there was a contretemps on board or shortly after his arrival because he celebrated his return to the mother country by spending three days in the glasshouse for insolence at Shorncliff.

Sharp was in the Canadian Army Medical Corps and served in different hospitals before being despatched to the Kitchener Hospital, Brighton on 5 March 1917. The Kitchener Hospital was established in 1915 in premises belonging to the Poor Law Institution and for a while served as an Indian Military Hospital staffed with British surgeons and doctors from the Indian Medical Service based at Peshawar. By the time Sharp arrived at Brighton the Indians had been relocated to other hospitals in the area and the Kitchener Hospital was full of British and Dominion soldiers.

By 1917 David Sharp was serving in the Canadian Army Service Corps when he was sent to the Kitchener Hospital, Brighton. In this group, he is the second man to the right of the three nurses. (D. Sharp)

This nurse also worked in the Kitchener Hospital. Her photograph was among Sharp's souvenirs and so perhaps she was important to him at the time. (D. Sharp)

On the back of this postcard is a handwritten note: 'Some of the boys at the Kitchener Hospital.' The nurse wears a splendid military greatcoat. Is it hers or did she borrow it? (D. Sharp)

On the back of this postcard a handwritten note states: 'Section of the St John Ambulance serving the Indian General Hospital, York Place.' (D. Sharp)

Later on in 1917, Sharp did look after Indian soldiers in the Indian Military Hospital at York Place, which occupied school premises. One of his turbaned patients was called Ramber and a postcard portrait of him was amongst Sharp's souvenirs. Another treasured postcard was of a pretty nurse with a tiny waist who may or may not have been a sweetheart. Sharp also did a stint at the Military Hospital based in the newly built Brighton, Hove and Sussex Grammar School at Hove.

Not far away from York Place was a newsagent's shop in Clyde Road run by a competent but lovely young lady by the name of Mabel Perrin. She ran the shop on behalf of her father who had three shops in Brighton. Sharp fell in love with Mabel and he must have been a fast mover because only five months after arriving in Brighton he was thinking of marriage. Hasty wartime marriages were nothing new but he was still under military discipline and needed to obtain permission from his superiors. This was granted on 24 July 1917. Legally he was not yet an adult and should have had his father's permission too, but the happy couple married on 2 September 1917 at St Saviour's Church, Brighton.

Later on in 1917 Sharp went to the Indian Military Hospital in York Place and Ramber, pictured here, was one of the patients. (D. Sharp)

David Sharp also worked at the Second Eastern Military Hospital in Dyke Road, Hove. This photograph is of King's Ward.
(D. Sharp)

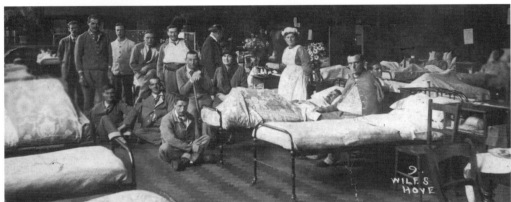

Another of the Dyke Road wards is seen here in 1916. One soldier is fortunate enough to have a female visitor, perhaps his wife or mother. (D. Sharp)

Sharp kept this postcard and the one above to remind him of those days although the photographs were taken before he arrived at Brighton. On 21 August 1915 a section of the Royal Army Medical Corps line-up on the steps before leaving for service overseas. (D. Sharp)

Sharp was the recipient of two British war medals. This was unusual but then he had served for two separate periods. In 1919 David and Mabel Sharp were despatched to a special discharge depot for married couples in Buxton, Derbyshire. The establishment was called the Granville Canadian Special Hospital and they arrived there on 10 February. Then they travelled to Liverpool and sailed to Canada aboard the SS *Grampian*. Oddly enough it was the same vessel in which he had first sailed from Canada in 1915 – perhaps he recognized some of the crew. The couple

Sharp fell in love with Mabel Perrin, who managed a newsagent's shop in Clyde Road, Brighton. (D. Sharp)

David Sharp and his wife on board the SS Grampian in 1919 en route for Canada. (D. Sharp)

David Sharp married Mabel Perrin on 2 September 1917 at St Saviour's Church, Brighton. The wedding cake is interesting because the decoration appears to include a 'V for Victory' at the base. (D. Sharp)

This picture records a spectacular costume Mabel Perrin wore in her younger days. Perhaps it was created for a carnival or other special occasion but whatever the event a great deal of work was necessary. (D. Sharp)

arrived at St John on 10 March and from there it was a slog of almost 2,000 miles by train and ferry to reach Winnipeg. Once there he completed his formal discharge from the Army on 5 April 1919. The Sharps attempted to settle down in Winnipeg but somehow they could not manage to do so and by 1920 were back in Brighton where their first child was born, followed by five more born in Brighton and two born in Portslade.

Dublin-born Revd Vicars Armstrong Boyle was vicar of St Nicolas Church, Portslade, from 1899 to 1919. He was a friend of Revd Samuel Augustus Barnett (founder of Toynbee Hall, a pioneering welfare settlement in the east end of London) and his formidable wife Dame Henrietta Barnett (founder of Hampstead Garden Suburb). In 1913 the couple retired to Hove and when they died were buried in St Helen's Churchyard, Hangleton. Boyle was also rector of this parish. Boyle lived in the Portslade vicarage with his sister who was a great help to him in his ministry. Unusually, they were both strong supporters of the women's suffrage movement.

Boyle's first cousin was the famous Lieutenant Commander Edward Courtney Boyle RN, who was awarded a Victoria Cross for his exploits in the troubled waters of the Dardanelles and lived to tell the tale. He was in command of the submarine E-14 and on 27 April 1915 managed to negotiate his vessel into the forbidden area of the Sea of Marmara. This was no easy task because E-14 had to dive down and travel carefully underneath a minefield. Once in the Sea of Marmara he set about his wartime task, sinking the *Murel Bahr*, a Turkish gunboat, and

The vessel featured here was captioned the 'new E-class type submarine'. Lieutenant Commander Edward Courtney Boyle was awarded a Victoria Cross for his exploits aboard submarine E-14. (Author)

sending a torpedo into the *Peik/Sheket*. Fittingly, the whole crew was decorated, the lieutenant and acting-lieutenant receiving a Distinguished Service Cross and the ratings being awarded Distinguished Service Medals.

Boyle ventured on two more submarine missions without mishap. But E-14 earned her own particular niche in naval history because a subsequent captain was also awarded a VC, only his came posthumously. The vessel came under heavy fire and was so near to safe waters but sank off the Turkish coast in January 1918. Although there were thirty-two survivors, twenty-five lives were lost. In 2012 the site of the wreck was located.

Meanwhile, in 1916 Lieutenant Commander Boyle was home on leave and visited his priestly cousin in Portslade. He was persuaded to present certificates for good attendance and good conduct to some scholars at St Nicolas Girls' School. The girls were suitably impressed to see a hero in person.

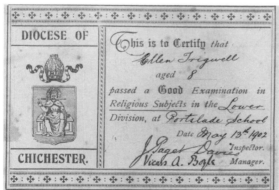

This certificate issued in 1902 for a good exam result in religious studies was probably similar in design and format to the ones given out by Lieutenant Commander Boyle in 1916 for good attendance and good conduct. (Author)

Lieutenant Commander Boyle survived the Great War and indeed went on to serve in World War II. He died aged 94 in 1967, having ended his career as a rear admiral.

In 1908 Arthur Gates became a teacher at St Nicolas School, Portslade and in 1912 Gladys Austen joined the staff. They continued to be fellow teachers until 1914 when Gates was called up – he had already joined the Territorial Force. Gladys was friendly with the rest of the Gates family as well but there was no special 'understanding' between her and Arthur when he went off to war. In 1917 he was home on leave and visited his old friends at the school. Portslade resident Mr

Still had the surprise of his life somewhere near the Front in France when a dispatch rider slid to a halt near him and it turned out to be Arthur Gates.

After the war Gates was demobbed with the rank of second lieutenant. Once safely home he asked his mother if Gladys was spoken for and his mother told him she was not but he had better get a move on. The couple married in 1921. Like so many returning soldiers, Gates was unsettled by his experiences and was restless in Portslade. He took a post in Cologne and Gladys travelled with him as a newly married woman. But they did not put down roots in Germany either and soon returned to England.

Second Lieutenant Arthur Gate was a schoolmaster before joining the Army. (D. Gedye)

They lived in a house in Boundary Road, Hove, and Gates taught at St Andrew's School, Portslade. Arthur Gates was a man of some talent who enjoyed playing a violin and harp. He excelled at woodwork, teaching the subject to the boys at St Andrew's and indulging in woodcarving as a hobby. He carved hymn boards for local churches and inscribed the names of Old Boys on the backs of chairs in Lancing College Chapel. In 1922, when Gladys was already 35 years old, she gave birth to their first child Muriel. Don followed in 1924. The following year Gates was struck down by pneumonia and did not recover. He died on 30 November 1925. Three months after his death, their third child Graham was born. Arthur Gates lived on in the memory of boys he once taught and one of them became very famous indeed. He was Fred Miles who, with his brother George, designed aircraft in the early days of aviation. In June 1918 the children at St Andrew's School were given a special holiday to celebrate the feat of Old Boy Gordon Miles who had escaped from a prisoner-of-war camp. But it is not clear whether or not he was a member of the remarkable Miles family. Meanwhile Gladys was obliged to return to a full-time teaching post to provide for herself and her children.

Mr R. Winters was another teacher from St Nicolas School who served in the Great War and he joined the Royal Naval Volunteer Reserve. Like Gates he was fortunate to return from the war and in

1919 resumed teaching at the school. He particularly enjoyed taking his class on nature study rambles over the Downs. But perhaps, like Gates, his war duties had sapped his strength, and he too died suddenly in 1925. Their names do not appear on any war memorial but it could be said they were victims of war and so too were the three fatherless Gates children.

Frederick Peters and his family lived at 29 Elm Road, Portslade, and he was foreman of the paint shop at Portslade Gas Works. The family consisted of husband and wife, three sons and a daughter plus a step-sister from Peters' first marriage. The couple must have had a great shock when Mrs Peters became pregnant at the age of 45 and the father was ten years older. Cecil was born in 1915 and was too young to remember his big brother, another Frederick Peters who went away to fight with the East Surrey Regiment. Tragically, he was killed on 1 November 1918, ten days before the Armistice.

The colliers bringing coal from north-east England to Portslade Gasworks were given appropriate names. Thus *Portslade* was one and the *F.E. Webb* and *John Miles* were two others, named in honour of Gas Company directors. On 22 February 1917 the SS *John Miles* sailed from Jarrow on Tyne with her holds packed with 870 tons of coal. But she never made it to Portslade. The German submarine U-21 sent a torpedo into her port side and she went down within two minutes. No doubt the fact that the vessel was fully laden did not help the situation and there was no time for the fourteen-strong crew to make adequate preparations to abandon ship. Nine of the crew were drowned and the five survivors were left struggling to stay afloat by clutching at such wreckage as they could

Private Fred Peters of the 1/East Surrey Regiment was only 19 when he was killed in action on 22 October 1918. The Peters family lived at 29 Elm Road, Portslade. (C. Peters)

lay hands on. Fortunately, within a short while, a British minesweeper came to the rescue and put the men ashore at Hartlepool. But the ordeal was too much for Second Engineer Robert Slater Wilkinson, aged 54 who died on board the minesweeper. He was buried in Portslade Cemetery. He and his wife Ellen lived at 7 North Street, Portslade.

An inquest was held for three crewmen from the SS *John Miles*, namely Thomas Brazier, chief officer, from Shoreham, Robert Wilkinson from Portslade and Andrew Atkinson, donkey-man (in the merchant navy this term meant he was in charge of the donkey engine as well as being something of a jack-of-all-trades). Survivor Seaman William Phillips said at the inquest: 'All the hatches were blown off by the explosion and the starboard lifeboat was filled with coal.' The verdict was that the deaths were due to drowning in the North Sea through the sinking of the ship by a hostile mine. The truth about the torpedo was not established until later on.

Another Portslade victim from the SS *John Miles* was Steward Emmanuel Tester, aged 61. He and his wife Ellen lived at 72 Trafalgar Road. Also lost was Master Mariner Thomas Vallint, who was born in North Shields on 8 April 1875 but later lived at 4 St Leonard's Terrace, Aldrington. But when his widow Mrs E.E. Vallint filled out the service record card she gave her address as 57 George Scott Street, South Shields, Durham.

The location where SS *John Miles* sank was 11 miles south-east of Hartlepool. In August 2007 members of a sub-aqua club discovered the brass ship's bell and brought it to the surface. It was inscribed with the ship's name, the date 1908 (when she was built) and London (where she was registered).

Sidney Chappell enlisted in the 1/Royal Sussex Regiment in 1903. For an ordinary local lad it proved an eye-opening experience because he travelled the world at His Majesty's expense and saw service in Malta, Crete, Belfast and India. In fact his battalion was still stationed in India when the time for home leave came up in 1914. He travelled back with exotic souvenirs in the shape of a fine shawl and a parrot. Since there was plenty of free time aboard ship, he managed to teach the parrot some English words and phrases. But he was careful the parrot should not acquire swear words because he did not want to upset the sensibilities of his female relatives. During his leave in Sussex he fell in love with an Irish girl and proposed marriage. She obviously needed time to make up her mind about such an important step. When his leave was up, instead of being sent back to India to rejoin his comrades, he was sent to France and he had to embark not knowing what her answer would be. She then sent him a letter turning him down. It is not known if he ever received or read it because he was killed on active service at Vendresse on 14 September 1914.

Sidney Chappell had a sister called Lucy who married Alfred Ford. The couple went on to have six children. At first they lived in Cowper Street, Hove, but in 1903 they moved to a house in Wolseley Road, Portslade. This was because the second child, William, was considered rather delicate and their doctor advised a move. Whether the Portslade air was more salubrious or

Sidney Chappell was a regular soldier before war broke out, having enlisted in 1905 in the 1/Royal Sussex Regiment. He was killed at Vendresse on 14 September 1914. (Mrs Marriot)

not, the fact was that William grew up strong and healthy enough to join the Royal Navy and become a chief petty officer. But he did give his family a bad fright in 1918 when he became very ill with Spanish Flu. By that time the family had moved to more spacious premises in Norway Street, Portslade, as the arrival of the fifth child, Kathleen, in 1914 meant they were somewhat overcrowded in the old place. Then there was a gap until the sixth and last child, Doris, arrived in 1920. This was because Alfred Ford enlisted in the Royal Engineers. Lucy must have found it very hard to cope on her own with five children, along with the privations and scarcity of food in wartime. Although Alfred returned home safely from war, the final baby proved to be just too much for poor Lucy who died suddenly aged 41, six weeks after the birth. The burden of housekeeping and looking after the children then fell on her daughter Edith, who was obliged to leave work and give up her independence. Later on the accumulated strain of those years caught up with Edith and she was

In November 1917, Alfred Ford of the Royal Engineers was photographed with his wife Lucy and children Ethel, Harry and Edith in the back row, and Kathleen and Sid in front. (Mrs Marriot)

ill for two years. Alfred Ford married a widow with four children in 1935 and the children from the first marriage felt sidelined.

The Forrest family lived at 9 St Andrew's Road, Portslade. Charles Ernest Forrest was a printer by trade, having been apprenticed to the well-known firm of Emery whose premises were situated on the corner of Vallance Road and Church Road, Hove, and where the *Hove Echo* was printed. He and his wife Charlotte Mary had one child born in 1914, a son called Reg by everyone. Her husband enlisted in the Royal Garrison Artillery and was away much of the time, including a spell in Salonika, but he survived the war.

Reg was only 3 years old when one vivid memory imprinted itself firmly on his mind. He was happily playing in North Street with other children when suddenly two British planes collided overhead and pieces of metal and scraps of fuselage clattered down on the road all around them. The following extract was printed in the *Brighton and Hove Gazette* (23 May 1917):

Charles Ernest Forrest was a printer by trade before he served in the Royal Garrison Artillery. In this 1916 photograph he stands behind his wife, Charlotte Mary, and their son Reg, who is still young enough to be clad in a dress. (R. Forrest)

A distressing tragedy of the air was witnessed at Hove, yesterday evening, resulting in the death of two young officers of the Royal Flying Corps. Shortly after six o'clock four aeroplanes were high up near the western border of Hove, nearly to Portslade. The evening was beautifully calm, with practically ideal conditions for air tactics. Suddenly two of the machines collided. One fell a shapeless mass in Marine Park (Aldrington Recreation Ground) the exact spot being at the western end and towards the south-west of the enclosure, where the engine partially embedded itself in the fresh green turf; while the other came down on the sands opposite Hove Seaside Villas, a residential terrace of houses which stands right on the foreshore. Each machine had one occupant. The officer who was piloting that which descended on the park was terribly injured and dead, but his hands still grasped the steering wheel. Amongst the broken parts of the other machine, its pilot also lay dead, having been instantaneously killed [...] For a little while after the collision portions of the machines descended to earth at various parts, a portion of the tail of one being found in the churchyard of St Leonard's Church [...] pieces were also picked up in Worcester Villas and other places.

Second Lieutenant Cyril Frederick Crapp, Royal Flying Corps was buried in St Leonard's Churchyard.
(Author)

The dead officers were Second Lieutenant William John Douglas Vince, who joined the Air Service in June 1916, and Second Lieutenant Cyril Frederick Crapp, who joined in July 1916.

Both airmen are commemorated on the War Memorial inside St Leonard's Church and Second Lieutenant Crapp was buried in the churchyard, near the south-west wall and for many years a piece of the wreckage rested on top of his tombstone. Eric Holden, who was 5 years and 10 months old at the time, witnessed the collision and together with other boys rushed to the spot where they thought a plane had crashed. But the gates of the recreation ground had already been closed and the boys peered through the cracks to see the wrecked plane. Then they went to the seashore and saw the second plane on the sand, it being low tide. There was a policeman on duty there to keep people away.

Reg Forrest's second vivid memory of the Great War was of the terrific noise that accompanied the celebration of Armistice Day. The explosion of fireworks and bangers gave him such a fright that he bolted from the scene and dived into a bed occupied by a kindly neighbour.

John Tidy was born from his mother's first marriage and when she re-married she became Mrs Jenner. They lived at 50 High Street, Portslade, one of those old flint-built cottages. John Tidy earned his living as a maintenance engineer at the Petersfield Laundry on Old Shoreham Road. It was a large enterprise and provided work for many local people including Daisy Blaber, Tidy's future bride.

Mrs Jenner suffered heartbreak in the Great War when she lost her 17-year-old son Ernest Tidy. He was aboard HMS *Viknor* when the vessel sank on 13 January 1915.

John Tidy also served in the war with the Royal Horse Artillery. Although he returned home in one piece, his eardrums had been shattered by the noise of exploding shells. He was thus rendered totally deaf. His mother assumed he would be unable to hold down an ordinary job and so she purchased a smallholding for him at Mile Oak. He was grateful for her concern and he certainly kept hold of the smallholding. But he was also determined to get his old job back at the laundry and with persistence he managed it.

John Tidy relied on lip-reading and his wife Daisy learned sign language so that she could communicate with him when he was unable to understand what was said. He needed people to face him and speak clearly if he was to lip-read properly but often people did not realize his difficulties. It was frustrating when people treated him like an imbecile and talked across him to address his wife. Particularly annoying were questions such as 'Does he take sugar?' He turned his affliction to his advantage, however. When the couple had a quarrel, Daisy could shout as much as she liked. He would simply turn his head away and close his eyes.

The couple shared the old cottage with his mother. Space was limited at the best of times but when a daughter, Betty, was born, and later a son, the cottage was full to

This portrait of Jack Tidy and his wife Daisy was taken in the 1920s by Portslade photographer H.W. Tubbs. (B. Figg)

bursting point. There were only two bedrooms upstairs and Mrs Jenner shared her large iron and brass bedstead with her grand-daughter Betty while the Tidys and their son squashed into the other bedroom. There was an outdoor privy and water was drawn from the well. On Saturday evenings the tin bath was unhooked from the wall outside and brought into the warmth of the scullery for family bath-night. The youngest child had the privilege of clean water and John was the last one in.

In 1914 the War Office took over the playing fields of Windlesham House School in Portslade. It must have been mortifying for Mrs Charles Scott Malden, the owner and manager of the school, because she had only just moved the establishment from its previous home at Brighton in 1913. Moreover, a great deal of effort had been put into preparing the playing fields for football and cricket. They needed to be levelled and the ubiquitous flints dug out. The precious turf on the cricket field was carefully removed from its old home and relaid at Portslade. Then the Army arrived and pitched their white bell-shaped tents. The boys of course thought it was very exciting and were more than willing to help in the erection of the tents. Then there were the 600 mules quartered for a spell while awaiting shipment to the Dardanelles, where many of the unfortunate creatures perished.

The camp also became a magnet for the local children who would hang about the gap in the hedge at Locks Hill hoping the soldiers were in a generous mood. George Steele remembered fondly the large tin of

There was great local interest in military camps and so it is not surprising that so many photographs were taken, with this being of the Royal Engineers in 1914. (J. Hayward)

The 11th Royal Warwick occupied the site c. 1915. Loxdale can be seen in the background. The rows of bell tents look splendid but at a later date there was so much rainfall that the camp was flooded. (R. Jeeves)

Australian apricot jam he was given, which was a great treat for the family. Another time he was given a loaf of bread, which he quickly concealed under his blue school jumper and ran all the way home.

A prolonged spell of bad weather caused the campsite to become flooded and soldiers were moved out to drier accommodation in neighbouring houses. Residents did not exactly volunteer hospitality but the Army authorities visited houses to check on the amount of space available. Their privacy might have been invaded but there were advantages because a lodging fee of one shilling a day per soldier was paid and there were extra rations too. George Steele's family played host to three soldiers who shared one bed in the middle bedroom while his baby sister was moved into her parents' room, and George and his brother were squashed together in the small bedroom known as the slip room. The soldiers were not much trouble because they were gone early in the morning and were away most of the day. Payday became quite

The 91st Field Company Royal Engineers were at Portslade in 1915. (Author)

Soldiers from the camp were photographed in c. 1916 in what was known as the Locks Hill Plantation where the children came to gather beechnuts. (Mrs Marriot)

a spectacle. The paymaster marched to their billets accompanied by soldiers bearing a folding table and chair. These were plonked on the pavement, then the dignified paymaster took his seat and the soldiers lined up smartly to receive their pay. When new Army huts were erected at the campsite, the soldiers left their lodgings.

The 24 Signal Company Royal Engineers were photographed in camp at Portslade in 1914 with the cookhouse staff in cheerful mood. Later on cooking became more serious when an Army School of Cookery was established here. (Author)

But the Reed family, who lived in Southwick, had soldiers billeted on them throughout the war. The Reeds like the Steeles were market gardeners, which was a bonus in a time of food shortages because they never went short of vegetables even when it was impossible to buy potatoes in the shops. Later on Florence Reed married George Steele.

In around 1916 the campsite became the Army School of Cookery. In April 1918 it was stated that around 14,000 army cooks had qualified there during the previous two years. According to Directories the Army School of Cookery was still there in 1924.

Hove Council cast envious eyes on the thirty-eight stout army huts at the site. They thought they would be a marvellous stop-gap during the housing crisis. The huts could be purchased for around £66 each and it would only cost £250 to convert a single hut into two dwellings. In 1919 the Army was willing to give up seven huts immediately but the landowners, the trustees of the late Mr F.E.J. Blackburne-Hall, refused to countenance such an idea.

The boys and girls of St Nicolas School, Portslade, played their part in easing the food shortages. The Ministry of Food, with the blessing of the Education Committee, organized an expeditionary force of schoolchildren in October 1918 to go to the Downs and pick blackberries. The boys picked 7cwt and 14lb and the girls picked nearly 5cwt and 17lb. The fruit was sold to the Maison-le-Bry jam factory in Vale Road, Portslade, at three pennies a pound. The sum of sixteen pounds, thirteen shillings and three pence was then distributed amongst the delighted children.

Portslade Industrial School was constructed on the Downs at an estimated cost of £30,000. But the money did not come from Portslade because it was a joint venture between London County Council and Brighton Council. The school was built to a high standard and had its own gymnasium and swimming pool with bathrooms and shower rooms close by. The bedrooms were on the first floor. The site had the advantage of plenty of fresh air, and this together with cleanliness, firm discipline, exercise and practical training was felt to be the best way forward to sort out troubled boys. The boys who were sent there were either beyond the control of their parents, or had been convicted of an offence that would normally require a prison sentence.

Several boys from Portslade Industrial School who trained in the brass and reed band, went on to join the Army as musicians. (Author)

On arrival each boy was issued with a jersey, a tweed coat, a military overcoat, two shirts, two flannel vests, woollen stockings, a pair of boots and a pair of slippers. On Sundays they wore a blue serge suit and cap. There were practical lessons in boot making, carpentry and tailoring. The school had its own smallholding and in 1906 there were three cows, a horse and some pigs. Pigs continued to be kept until the 1950s.

The brass and reed band was of a high standard. Indeed, the visiting bandmaster, Mr G. Jamieson, earned more than anyone else employed at the school with the exception of the superintendent, one master and the farm bailiff. The band provided the music for many local events and the boys were glad to mix with ordinary people and get away from discipline for a while. It is not surprising that many boys joined the Army as musicians.

In the early days a record was kept of which regiments boys joined with the name in brackets indicating where that regiment was stationed:

3rd Lancashire Fusiliers (Barbados)
1st King's Own Lancaster Rifles (Malta)
4th Manchester Regiment (Cork)
Royal Naval School of Music (Portsmouth)
4th Lancashire Fusiliers (Ireland)
4th Rifle Brigade (Chatham)
1st East Lancashire Regiment (Dublin)
Royal Engineers (Aldershot)
4th Hussars (Ireland)
Welsh Fusiliers (India)
1st Manchester Regiment (Singapore)

It was inevitable that some Old Boys would become caught up in the Great War and the Roll of Honour inside St Nicolas Church, Portslade, lists the names of twenty-seven who died – two at least were bandsmen. They were Bandsman Albert Chase of the 4/Rifle Brigade, who was killed in action on 14 May 1915, and Bandsman William Glazier of the 2/West Yorkshire Regiment, who was killed in action on 12 January 1915. Perhaps the saddest case was Private Morgan Henry Mason of the 1/Welsh Regiment who was only 16 when he was killed in action at Ypres on 25 May 1915 – a short and troubled life. In contrast Private Thomas Newman was a reservist serving with the Royal Sussex Regiment when he was killed in action at Richebourg L'Avoue on 9 May 1915. Mysteriously, there seems to be no official military information concerning nine of the names on the Roll of Honour and there is doubt about another two. The Industrial School must have had information that has since been lost.

The Smiths were an important Portslade family being involved with the Britannia Steam Mills for many years. The 1861 census recorded Charles R. Smith, miller, living near the Halfway House pub. His two older sons, Frederick and Richard, eventually took over the business. By this time Frederick Sundius Smith had become active in local affairs. He was a Portslade councillor from 1894 to 1908 and a trustee of Shoreham Harbour, besides being chairman of the finance committee of both bodies. He was an overseer of the poor at Portslade and instrumental in establishing the first public day school in Portslade. He habitually wore a wing collar and sported a droopy moustache.

By 1891 he and his wife Emily Beatrice lived at Courtenay House, Courtenay Terrace Portslade, with a cook, housemaid, nurse and under-nurse. Their family consisted of five sons and two daughters. The firstborn was Beatrice Muriel who in 1908 married Captain Frederick Roper Holbrooke (later Lieutenant Colonel) of the Indian Army, son of Revd F.G. Holbrooke, Vicar of Portslade. Gladys Dorothy was born in 1890 and died the following year. The sons were Basil Knightley Sundius Smith (1887-1959) Walter Frederick Sundius Smith (1889-1969) Colonel Donald Geoffrey Sundius Knightley Smith, 1/15th Punjab Regiment Indian Army (1892-1986), and Lieutenant Colonel Brian Leslie Sundius Smith, DSO, Baluch Regiment Indian Army (1895-1965).

The other son born in 1894 was Second Lieutenant Ronald Christian

Sundius Smith, Indian Army attached to the 2/West Yorkshire Regiment, who was killed in action at Neuve Chappelle on 12 March 1915 aged 20. There is a stained-glass window in his memory at St Andrew's Church, Portslade. The window depicts St George and was created from the designs of Sir Edward Burne-Jones and manufactured by William Morris & Co.

The area of Portslade south of Old Shoreham Road known variously as Copperas Gap, Southern Cross and Portslade-by-Sea, is a compact area of dense housing. It is possible to realize the dreadful impact of Great War losses on this close-knit community by looking at some figures where it

The beautiful stained glass window of St George was the creation of Sir Edward Burne-Jones and the William Morris Company. It commemorates Second Lieutenant Ronald Christian Sundius Smith, who was killed in action on 12 March 1915. (Author)

Residents of Trafalgar Road suffered the death of several brave men in the Great War. (Author)

seems there was not a street that did not have its own tragedy. In Trafalgar Road there were at least nine losses:

Number 42 – Private William Watkin Wynn, died at home 19 August 1916

Number 56 – Private John Harold Curtis Wareham, killed in action 9 May 1915

Number 70 – Private Albert George Booker, killed in action 31 July 1917

Number 72 – Steward Emmanuel Tester, SS *John Miles*, drowned 22 February 1917

Number 74 – Guardsman Percy Steele, killed in action 26 December 1916

Number 76 – Private Ernest George Pratt, died of dysentery 13 December 1918

Number 87 – Private William James Timms, killed in action 25 March 1918

Number 132 – Lance Sergeant Neil Murray Campbell, killed in action 30 September 1918

Number 143 – Private Albert Frank Strevens, killed in action 3 September 1917

From Eastbrook Road, Wellington Road and Wolseley Road there were four deaths in each. From East Street and St Andrew's Road there were three deaths in each. From Abinger Road, Bampfield Street, Brambledean Road, Church Road, Crown Road, Gardner Street, George Street, Middle Street and Station Road there were two deaths in each. Other roads suffered a single death.

Even in Portslade Old Village with just a few houses in High Street, there were three losses:

Number 45 – Private William George Lindup, killed in action 19 September 1918

Number 48 – Corporal Alfred George Robinson, killed in action 17 May 1915

Number 50 – Able Seaman Ernest Tidy, HMS *Viknor*, drowned 13 January 1915

It is quite possible these figures might not reflect the true scale because the exact address of the fallen was not always recorded.

CHAPTER 6

Brothers in Arms

Walter Smith Baddeley came originally from Manchester. By the 1890s he had settled in Portslade-by-Sea, where he kept a grocery shop in North Street, which in those days was the principal shopping area of Portslade. He made a good living and left over £3,000 when he died in 1935. Walter Smith Baddeley's father James Baddeley started off as an agricultural labourer but worked his way up in the world until by the time he died in 1902 he was living in Boothend Farm, near Worsley, having carried on the business of a tea merchant at a wonderfully-named address, 4 Hanging Ditch, Manchester. Not content with that he was also a licensed victualler at the High Turk's Head, Shudehill, Manchester.

Walter Smith Baddeley married Agnes Louisa Cousins, who had been employed as a draper's assistant. They had a family of four children, all born in Portslade. The eldest child born in 1892, was Agnes Louisa, named after her mother, then came Walter Hubert Baddeley born in 1894, followed by Margaret Hannah born in 1896 and lastly the baby of the family, Alfred James Baddeley born in 1899. His relatives called the elder son Hubert, probably to distinguish him from his father, but his professional name was always Walter. The younger son was habitually called Jim.

The family attended St Andrew's Church in Church Road, Portslade, and Walter became a Sunday School teacher there. The brothers were educated at Varndean School, Brighton.

The Baddeley boys had fond memories of their boyhood days and when Walter Baddeley was a well-travelled and successful man, he

Walter Hubert Baddeley was a Sunday-school teacher at St Andrew's Church, Portslade. (Author)

made a radio broadcast in June 1945 evoking a magic picture of times past:

> We boys used to go down to the beach after school or in the holidays and there we'd see the fishermen standing in groups along the shore, their boats all ready at the water's edge, nets piled in the stern, oars in rowlocks. The fishermen standing, shading their eyes, looking out to sea, searching for the signs of a shoal approaching. Then suddenly the cry would go up. The men rushed their boats down into the sea, jumped in, and then, as some rowed their hardest, others would pay out the net. The boat would make a big semi-circular sweep so that the shoal was enclosed within the net. We used to stand on the beach and watch. As the net was paid out, on the top of the water there gradually appeared a line of corks, which were fastened along one side of the net to keep it afloat.

The boys then lent a hand pulling in the nets and they would be given two or three mackerel, which made 'a very jolly supper on a cold evening'.

In 1912 at the Michaelmas term, Walter Hubert Baddeley embarked upon his studies at Keble College, Oxford. It was an unusual progression for a Portslade boy from an ordinary background and state education to aspire to the dreaming spires of Oxford. He must have been an exceptional student because he won a scholarship and went to Oxford with the support of the Grocers' Company. When war broke out in 1914 there was no need for him to interrupt his studies because he had not yet completed his degree. But he felt his duty lay with the Army and so he left the tranquillity of Oxford for war service.

Both brothers served in the Royal Sussex Regiment. Lieutenant Alfred James Baddeley of the 2nd Battalion was killed in action on 23 October 1918 and it must have been doubly upsetting for the family when they realized how close the date was to the Armistice. He was only 19. His name is inscribed on the memorial at Vis-en-Artois British War Cemetery at Harcourt in the Pas de Calais, on the road from Arras to Cambrai. On the day he died near Catillon there was a concerted British attack on German lines in the Valencienne area. Perhaps his family were too numb to think of a memorial at once and it was to be ten years before a beautiful three-light window was installed at St Andrew's Church, Portslade, depicting the Resurrection. Ward & Hughes of 67 Frith Street, Soho designed the window and the faculty was dated 21 June 1928. The window is still there but today it is placed as three separate windows in the chancel. Alfred's name was already on the wooden war memorial inside the church, instituted in 1921.

By contrast Hubert Walter Baddeley seemed

This stained glass window of the Resurrection is to be found in St Andrew's Church, Portslade, and commemorates Second Lieutenant Baddeley, who was killed in action on 23 October 1918. (D. Sharp)

to lead a charmed life and indeed as it was later remarked he was 'The

Right Man in the Right Place at the Right Time'. His war record was exemplary and he was on active service from July 1915 to 1918. He was present at the battle of the Somme and came through unscathed when so many men died. In May 1917 he was Mentioned in Despatches no less than four times and was awarded the Military Cross the same year for his actions at Arras. The citation in the *London Gazette* (16 August 1917) went as follows:

> For conspicuous gallantry and devotion to duty. Whilst engaged in digging operations his company suddenly came under intense hostile barrage. His company commander and many others were killed. He at once took command, showing the utmost coolness and disregard of personal safety, and it was due to his example that a most difficult and urgent piece of work was completed.

In June 1918 he won a second Military Cross for his actions at St Quentin's. He was promoted to the rank of major and attached to the 8/East Surrey Regiment. He also served as an acting lieutenant colonel. In 1919 he was awarded the Distinguished Service Order and bar. He retired from the Army in April of that year and by September was back at his studies at Keble College, Oxford. He became president of the Oxford University Archaeological Society. Afterwards he attended Cuddesdon Theological College and was ordained a priest in 1921. He stayed in the Diocese of Yorkshire serving as curate and priest.

He became the seventh Bishop of Melanesia in 1932 and was consecrated on 30 November at St Mary's Cathedral, Parnell, New Zealand. He must have chosen the appropriate day himself because it was the feast day of St Andrew to remind him of his old church at Portslade. Another reminder of his boyhood was that the ship in which he visited the various islands was called the *Southern Cross* and of course there was an area called Southern Cross at Portslade. But how different was this small area compared with his enormous diocese covering a scattering of islands set in 90,000 square miles of the Pacific Ocean.

The bishop certainly did not choose the name *Southern Cross* himself as it followed a tradition of ships with the name dating back at least to the 1880s. The ship he used was in fact *Southern Cross VII*. He should have used ship number six but unfortunately she was wrecked on her maiden voyage. It was a most unfortunate incident because the ship contained all sorts of supplies intended for the Melanesian Mission. The bishop was fond of his ship. He could not oversee his diocese properly and visit far-flung places without her. After the Second World War the *Southern Cross* was in need of a refit but so anxious was the bishop to have her speedily returned that he sent a characteristic message saying he did not care if she was painted pink but he required her as soon as possible.

On 13 November 1935, when he was aged 41, the bishop married Mary Katherine Thomas at Adelaide Cathedral. She was the daughter of the Right Reverend Arthur Thomas, Bishop of Adelaide. Their son, Martin, was born on 10 November 1936 and was the first white child to be born in the Solomon Islands. He grew up to become a priest too. A daughter, Bridget, was born in 1940.

The Right Reverend Walter Baddeley DSO, MC, MA, Bishop of Melanesia, photographed in 1943. (The Right Reverend Dr Terry Brown)

Walter Baddeley served as bishop until 1947 during a very difficult time. He was in the Solomon Islands when the Japanese invaded on 26 January 1942. He famously said 'I'm staying' but he had taken the precaution of sending his wife and children to safety in Adelaide. He carried on his ministry as best as he could, keeping well out of sight of the Japanese and retreating into the bush. The Americans recognized the work he carried out under Japanese occupation by awarding him the United States Medal of Freedom with Palm, another medal to add to his collection. By 1943 he was in close contact with troops from New Zealand and the USA and he became honorary chaplain to them. His war record was a byword amongst servicemen who felt he was one of them and understood their problems. In 1944 the bishop was created an

The people of Melanesia created this cross of abalone shells for their bishop. (D. Sharp)

honorary Doctor of Sacred Theology of Columbia University, New York for his work amongst the troops and for helping to sustain their morale.

Bishop Walter Baddeley died in 1960. In 1962 the north aisle of St Andrew's Church, Portslade, was altered to become a memorial to Bishop Baddeley, and his family donated to the church a treasured cross created by the people of Melanesia from abalone shells. The cross has a beautiful iridescent sheen. The people of Melanesia continue to honour him especially, as 6 February is a day set aside in their calendar to remember him.

Second Lieutenant John Leslie Bright was one of the first to answer Kitchener's famous call and he joined the 7/Royal Sussex. He was sent to France and commissioned with his battalion in August 1915. After a short leave he joined the 2/Royal Sussex but was killed in action aged 26 on 25 September 1915 in the great advance near Vermelles. On the very same day and in the same campaign his brother, Second Lieutenant Kenneth Coldwell Bright of the 7/Royal Sussex, was badly wounded in the head and invalided home. When he recovered he joined the 3/Royal Sussex, then attached to the 9/Royal Sussex and had barely become acclimatized to his new comrades when he was killed in action at Guillemont on 18 August 1916. His home address was 8 Bigwood Avenue and he had been an assistant in a wholesale ironmongery business but he did so well in the Army that he was promoted to sergeant in less than two months.

The Brooks family lived at 117 St Leonard's Avenue and their five sons all served in the Army. By 1918 one brother was a prisoner-of-war in Germany and three others were serving in France. The youngest, Private Arthur Neil of the Royal West Surrey Regiment, was killed in action on 12 August 1918. He worked for the *Brighton & Hove Society* and they published the following obituary:

> He was an apprentice to the Composing Department of the offices of this paper. He was a steady, persevering lad, and would have made a splendid workman, but on reaching the age of 18 was called to the colours. Only so recently as August 4 he sent a most cheerful letter to his late employers and a letter was sent in return wishing him 'all luck', but this letter apparently did not reach him, as the date on the letter was the actual day on which he made 'the great sacrifice', so that one more young life has been laid down in order that in future England shall be a better

land and free from the terrible menace of German aggression that has been our nightmare for years.

The Dickinson brothers were the sons of Captain Malcolm Dickinson of the Royal Artillery who lived at 25 Brunswick Terrace, and their grandfather was General Dickinson. Lieutenant John Malcolm Dickinson was educated at Marlborough and Sandhurst, and enlisted in the 2/Royal Sussex Regiment. He was killed in action on 12 June 1918 aged 20 and buried in Pernes British Cemetery. There is a brass memorial tablet to his memory in St Andrew's Church, Waterloo Street.

In the same church there is a memorial to his brother, Captain Thomas Malcolm Dickinson, who was born in 1893 and educated at Marlborough and Sandhurst. The memorial is unique in Hove and Portslade in setting out details of his military career and concludes with the heartfelt sentiment: 'A warrior *sans peur et sans reproche* – Valiant in Fight. Patient in Tribulation.'

Captain Dickinson and Lieutenant Dickinson are commemorated on memorial tablets inside St Andrew's Church, Waterloo Street, Hove. (Author)

In 1912 Captain Dickinson became a regular officer in the 16th Cavalry Indian Army but was later attached to the 1st Grenadier Guards. He was wounded in the left arm fighting at Festubert in May 1915. When he had recovered he was attached to the Royal Flying Corps and saw service in Mesopotamia. There he helped to provision the garrison at Kut in 1916. He was awarded the Distinguished Flying Cross for his 'excellent work in Mesopotamia'. He was also Mentioned in Despatches twice.

It is interesting to note that there was another local man at the siege of Kut. He was Able Seaman Walter Nye who was a veteran sailor, having served in the Royal Navy for twelve years. When he left the service he lived at 27 Franklin Road, Portslade, and became foreman of the Southern Counties Dairies, 146 Church Road Hove, whose manager was Mr J.F. Hunter. Nye re-enlisted in August 1914 and was assigned to HMS *Alert*. He was one of forty-nine sailors manning a horse-boat that conveyed equipment and supplies up the river for the Army. But when General Townshend decided to retreat from Ctesiphon, the Turks took the forty-nine sailors prisoner. Nye died of enteritis on 13 August 1916 while still in Turkish hands.

British and Indian troops were holed up in Kut surrounded by Turkish forces and were obliged to endure a siege with consequent famine conditions for 147 days. Although there were three British attempts to relieve Kut, none was successful. Meanwhile, food was scarce. By the end of February there were cases of scurvy and beri-beri and by April around thirty soldiers were dying daily from the effects of starvation. The Indian soldiers suffered badly because their caste forbade them from eating meat and the little milk available was reserved for patients in hospital. The British, meanwhile, ate any meat going with a preference for mule rather than horse, although a young donkey made a delectable meal and camel was not too tough and quite sweetish in taste. It must have been heartbreaking when an officer's favourite charger had to be butchered for the common good. But there was the dubious privilege of his mess being awarded the horse's heart and tongue.

The first British plane flew over Kut on 3 February 1916. But the planes were relatively primitive and quite unsuited for the task in hand. It was difficult to be accurate with their drops onto a small landing area because of the pilot's inexperience and gusty winds frequently meant the precious bundles fell into Turkish hands or were lost in the waters of the Tigris. The bundles weighed 80lb and to stop them from rocketing down too fast they were equipped with two white sheets, which as well as providing 'drag' also made them more visible to the hopeful soldiers below. All effort was in vain because the garrison at Kut surrendered on 29 April 1916. Some 2,500 British troops were taken captive and it is sad to record that only 700 returned home after the war. There were around 9,300 Indian troops at Kut and 2,500 of them died afterwards, like the British, on forced marches or in prisoner-of-war camps.

Another Hove man was also present at Kut. He was Captain John Alfred Tennant of the 14th Hussars. He served with the first force sent to relieve Kut (but failed) and was with the force that finally took Kut and Baghdad. He was born at Clifton in 1887 and educated at Winchester and Sandhurst. He lived at 22 The Drive. He was a professional soldier, having enlisted in December 1907. He served with the Mesopotamia Expeditionary Force from 1915 to 1918 and the North Persian Expeditionary Force from 1918 to 1919. In 1919 he was awarded the OBE (Military Division) for valuable services rendered in connection with military operations in Mesopotamia.

Meanwhile, Captain Dickinson had been deployed to France where he was wounded during air combat in June 1917 by receiving gunshot wounds to both legs. In 1917 on the Western Front he was taken prisoner. In 1918 he evacuated 6,000 British prisoners, 'being himself last to leave the fatal camp of Parchim'. But his experiences had taken their toll and his wounds were not healing properly. In Egypt he underwent an operation to try and correct the problems but died on the operating table on 4 June 1921. He was 27.

The surname Kekewich is certainly an unusual one and once heard it lingers in the memory. Lewis Pendarves Kekewich was born in 1859, the third son of Trehawke Kekewich of Peamore House, Exeter. Since he was neither heir nor spare, he was free to pursue his own life, which involved a business career in London. But he balanced city life with a keen interest in country pursuits such as hunting and shooting, and he also enjoyed a round of golf. His wife Lilian Emily was an excellent horsewoman too and a member of the Hunt. She was the daughter of Samson Hanbury of Bishopstone, Torquay, and the couple married on 2 October 1884. In 1909 Kekewich purchased Kidbrooke Park, Forest

Row, Sussex, for the sum of £35,000. But in later life they lived at Hove, firstly at 3 Beaumont Mansions, Fourth Avenue and then at 45 Brunswick Square. Kidbrooke Park was sold in 1916 to Sir James Horlick, the mastermind behind the famous hot drink.

The Kekewiches had a large family of seven children. There were three daughters, two of whom died in childhood, and four sons. But it is what happened to the four Eton-educated sons that tug at the heartstrings because only Sydney survived the Great War and he was severely injured. They had a military background because their uncle was Major General Robert George Kekewich of the Buffs (East Kent Regiment). Perhaps as youngsters they heard stirring stories of his military career with the South African War looming large, particularly the memorable Siege of Kimberley when their uncle was commander in charge of the beleaguered garrison.

The first son to die in the Great War was Captain John Kekewich of the Buffs, who was killed in action near Loos on 25 September 1915. It was not a straightforward death. He was involved in heavy fighting and wounded. But he refused to be rescued because he realized such an action would needlessly jeopardize the lives of his soldiers. He was posted missing. Before army service he had been a planter in the Malay States.

Captain George Kekewich was born on 20 July 1889. He was a London merchant and when he was at home in Kidbrooke Park was busy with the Boy Scout group he founded, being Master Scout. He

The names of the three Kekewich brothers are recorded on the brass memorial tablets in the lobby of Hove Library. (D. Sharp)

joined the City of London Yeomanry in September 1914 and was Mentioned in Despatches on 14 July 1917. He was serving in Palestine when he died on 28 October 1917 from wounds received the previous day at the Gaza Front. His estate amounted to £10,241. Nine days later the eldest son, Captain Hanbury Lewis Kekewich, who had served seven years in the Sussex Yeomanry and was also in Palestine, was killed in action near Sheria on 6 November 1917. That left Lieutenant Sydney Kekewich of the Lancers who was very badly wounded in September 1915. But he survived and continued to serve the Army, albeit in a safer environment with a desk job at the War Office's headquarters.

Widow Mrs Sarah Perrin of 20 Mortimer Road had three sons serving in the Army. Private Bert Perrin of the Middlesex Regiment was awarded the Military Medal in 1918. Private Dudley Perrin of the West Yorkshire Regiment was killed in action on 31 December 1917 and Private Arthur Hockley Perrin of the Royal Army Medical Corps was awarded the Military Medal in 1917. The latter was born at Brighton in 1893 but later lived at 96 Montgomery Street and was a fishmonger's assistant. He enlisted in August 1914.

David and Louisa Pinyoun lived at 16 Shirley Street and had a family of six sons. Mrs Pinyoun must have spent the most nerve-

The Pinyoun family lived at 16 Shirley Street. (Author)

Private Henry Pinyoun of the Royal Sussex Regiment died in Flanders on 26 June 1916. (D. d'Enno)

wracking years of any Hove woman during the Great War. Not only did her sons undertake war duties but also her 62-year old husband joined the colours, enlisting in November 1914 and by 1918 he was serving with the troops in Salonika. The eldest son, James, was a member of the Hove Defence Corps. The second son, Robert, had twelve years' service under his belt, eight at home and four in India – he also served on the frontier and in the South African war. The third son, Joseph, was an old member of the Hove Volunteers and by 1918 was on his way to India. The fourth son, David, had served in the Royal Navy for eighteen years by the end of the war and earned three good conduct stripes. The fifth son, Harry, joined the Royal Sussex Regiment and died in Flanders on 26 June 1916. The youngest son, Frederick, joined the Royal Marine Artillery. But Harry was the only one to be killed. A newspaper article wrote of Mrs Pinyoun, 'How to make ends meet is the constant care of the mother of this fine family.'

Major Poole had five sons serving in the armed forces. Major Poole was a veteran of the Crimean War and lived in Connaught Road. He was riding master at Eaton Riding Stables. His son, Private Ernest Albert Poole, was born in Brighton Barracks on 21 February 1870 and enlisted in November 1914. He joined the Royal Army Veterinary Corps and served in France for two years before contracting a disease and being honourably discharged on 4 November 1916. He died on 17 February 1917. Major Poole's other sons were: Rifleman Henry Poole, Rifle Brigade; Private Charles Poole, 7/Royal Sussex; Private William Poole, 2/6 Royal Sussex, in India; and Private John Poole, Royal Field Artillery. They all survived the war.

It was no surprise the Powell brothers should have a musical turn of mind because they were born in St Asaph, Denbighshire, and no doubt inherited the Welsh love of singing. Felix Lloyd Powell was the elder brother, being born in 1878, while George Henry Powell arrived in 1880.

In 1915 George Henry Powell had a sudden inspiration one morning while he was shaving and the lyrics of *Pack up your Troubles in your old Kit-bag* formed in his mind. He was in such a hurry to write down what he believed would be a winner that he rushed into the bedroom with lather still on his face, shouting to his wife, 'I've got it.' His brother Felix set the words to music and George's wife sang it at the Coliseum. But the song did not take off as hoped and, disappointed, they put it away. Later on during the war a competition was launched to find the best song to boost a nation's flagging morale. *Pack up your Troubles* was awarded first prize and ensured a steady flow of royalties for the brothers.

The brothers remained close despite a marked difference in their attitude to the Great War. While Felix became a Staff Sergeant, George was a pacifist, which did not matter too much until 1916 when the Military Act was passed. Up until then the Armed Forces consisted of regular personnel and volunteers but after such appalling losses conscription was inevitable. All men between the ages of 18 and 41 were called up and by April 1918 the manpower shortage was so acute men up to the age of 51 could be conscripted. It was a brave thing to be a pacifist, risking opprobrium from friends and neighbours, and then there was the ordeal of appearing before a tribunal to plead your case. The authorities saw to it that only a few were granted exemption; most of them being drafted into non-combatant roles such as stretcher-bearers. Refusal to comply carried the threat of a court martial. It is indeed ironic that the man who wrote such a world-famous military marching song should have been a pacifist. Perhaps this was the reason he published it under the pseudonym of George Asaf.

In 1921 George Henry Powell moved to Peacehaven where he and Felix quickly embraced community life by becoming involved in the monthly publication entitled *Peacehaven Post.* In fact George was the editor and the main force behind the venture. He was always quick to defend Peacehaven from criticism.

When the Second World War broke out, Felix joined the Peacehaven Home Guard. In 1942 he was aged 64 when he used his Home Guard rifle to shoot himself, while dressed in full uniform. Perhaps Peacehaven lost its charms for George after this loss and he spent the last ten years of his life at 10 Palmeira Avenue, Hove, where he died in December 1951.

In 1969 Richard Attenborough directed the film *Oh! What a Lovely War* and *Pack up your Troubles* was one of the wartime songs featured. You hear the song as wounded soldiers move along a railway platform. The final scenes would no doubt have met with pacifist George's approval because there is a dramatic panorama illustrating the utter waste of lives in war. It was shot from the sky and the camera pans over rows and rows of white crosses set out on the green Downs. The scene was set at Telscombe, which is not too far from Peacehaven, and because there had been a dry summer it was a taxing task to hammer 16,000 white crosses into the ground.

Mr and Mrs Donald Scobie had two sons and lived at 36 Pembroke Avenue. Mr Scobie had been employed in the civil service in India and his elder son John was born there in 1894, while the younger son Keith was born in Scotland. Both boys were awarded scholarships to Brighton College. John's was a mathematical scholarship but he was also keen on sports, winning three prizes at the College Athletic Sports Day and playing football and cricket for his house. He was a prefect and a sergeant in the college's Officers' Training Corps. He had a handful of Christian names, being John Angus Nicolson MacEwen (the last one was his mother's maiden name; she died in Burma in 1900). John went on to the Royal Military Academy, Woolwich, and in July 1914 enlisted in the Royal Engineers. He was promoted to lieutenant but was killed in action on 29 July 1916 with a bullet through the left lung. His brother Keith Macdonald Scobie had different interests at Brighton College, with strong literary tastes and was a leading member of the debating society. He took a keen interest in the college even after he left and hardly a term went by without him presenting some volumes to the college library. He too followed his brother to Woolwich from which he passed out first in May 1916. He served in France, including the Somme, for nine months before suffering a leg injury. In April 1917 he was sent home to recover, but it took some time for him to regain his strength. He too was promoted to lieutenant. In April 1918 he transferred to the Air Service. He had just completed his pilot's course with the RAF when on 27 October 1918 he was killed 'accidentally by an aeroplane' at Stockbridge Aerodrome.

Hugh Hamilton Scott was surveyor to the Hove Commissioners in the 1880s and fulfilled that function for a record forty-two years, including the transition to Hove Borough status. He was meticulous and hard-working and, it seems, diffident too. By 1918 he had been earning the same salary of £600 for fifteen years. When Hove councillors reviewed his pay, they stated he could have had a pay rise earlier if only he had asked.

But there was a romantic side to Scott too. He met Agnes Smith, daughter of a pastry cook, and they married after a whirlwind courtship. They set up home firstly in Waterloo Street and then at 44 Hova Villas.

The two Scott sons attended Hove High School in Clarendon Villas. Their father came from a strict Presbyterian background and the influence continued to exert itself in the family home. The blinds were kept drawn on the Sabbath Day and the only recreation permitted was bible study or the perusal of *Pilgrim's Progress*. Scott attended Cliftonville Congregational Church in Ventnor Villas until such time as a Presbyterian church (later known as St Cuthbert's) was established at Hove.

But his son Robert refused to follow him and remained at Cliftonville Congregational Church where a remarkable clergyman, Revd Ambrose Daniel Spong, presided for thirty-six years. He was a leading figure in Hove and the manner of his death was entirely in keeping with his lifestyle. On Christmas Day 1912 he preached at the Wesleyan Church in Portland Road, taking as his text the very same

The Scott family attended services in the building then known as the Cliftonville Congregational Church. (Author)

one he had used for his first sermon preached at the age of 16 in Shoreditch Workhouse, 'God so loved the world that He gave His only begotten Son.' After the service he hurried along to Hove Hospital to share dinner with the patients and then he returned home for the Christmas meal with his family. Not long afterwards he had a heart attack and died the same evening. There was a massive attendance at his funeral on 30 December. As the *Brighton Herald* put it:

> Rarely have the people of Hove been moved to such an expression of their grief as they were on this occasion – the interment of one who had lived and worked among them for 40 years, carrying the spirit of goodwill and loving service wherever he went.

Revd Ambrose Spong was related to H.H. Scott because Spong's daughter Winifred married Scott's son Robert in October 1915. By 1916 they were living in British Columbia where Robert was an architect. Robert enlisted as a private in the 72nd Canadian Battalion but was killed in action at Vimy Ridge on 1 March 1917 aged 33. Meanwhile Hugh, who had attended the University of London, was a civil engineer and lived with his wife at 19 Ventnor Villas. Hugh joined

The Scott brothers went to Hove High School in Clarendon Villas. The school war memorial is still to be seen next to the front door.
(Author)

the 25/Northumberland Fusiliers and was killed in action also at Vimy Ridge on 28 April 1917 aged 36. Both men were commemorated on the war memorial at their old school.

By 1916 Sergeant G. Sowter had served in the Hove Police for sixteen years. His sons were educated at George Street Schools and East Hove Schools. Leading Seaman George Sowter was in *Drake* Battalion, Royal Naval Division but was killed in action on 15 July 1915 aged 21. He was amongst the first landing party at Gallipoli and was shot by a sniper. His commanding officer wrote to his father:

Leading Seaman George Sowter was killed in action at Gallipoli on 15 July 1915.
(Hove Library)

Mr Cherry, who was killed in May and in whose platoon he was, always said that he was the most capable leading seaman he had. It will be some consolation for you to know, sir, that your son died doing his duty nobly, as he has never failed to do since the beginning of the campaign. We have lost in him a most brave and trustworthy hand and one we shall never be able to replace with another as he was one of the original Drake Battalion.'

Sergeant Sowter's second son, William Dewar Sowter, joined the 1/Cameron Highlanders before war broke out and was sent to France in August 1914. He rose through the ranks quickly and was promoted to sergeant major before the age of 21. He was awarded the Distinguished Conduct Medal: 'For conspicuous gallantry on September 15 1915 in the assault near Hulluch. As machine-gun sergeant of the battalion he handled his guns with the greatest bravery and dash during the latter stages of the assault, when both machine-gun officers had been wounded. With another non-commissioned officer he pushed on with one gun, and materially assisted the advance. While firing the gun the safety-catch was struck by a bullet, stopping the gun. Although under very heavy fire, he took out the damaged portion and continued to fire without it.'

In February 1916 he came home on leave and married Florence May Green at All Saints Church, Hove. The wedding cake was patriotically embellished with a machine-gun and the letters DCM. On 22 February 1916 Alderman A.R. Sargeant, Mayor of Hove, presented him with a handsome clock in appreciation of his services to King and Country, and as a token of good wishes for his marriage. It was pointed out that from Sowter's class of twenty boys at East Hove Schools, no less than eighteen of them were serving in the Army or the Navy.

There were once four Townsend brothers who lived at 56 Ellen Street, Hove. The three younger boys were all educated at Ellen Street Schools. The first brother to die in a conflict was Thomas Townsend who was killed in the Boxer

Sergeant Major William Dewar Sowter of the Cameron Highlanders received the Distinguished Conduct Medal. (Hove Library)

Rebellion in China in 1900. He died during the relief of Peking. John George Townsend joined the Royal Navy as a boy in 1890 and became a first class petty officer. He was aboard HMS *Viknor* when she went down on 13 January 1915 some 11 miles off the coast of Ireland, west of Tory Island, County Donegal. A mine may have struck the ship but there were also heavy seas at the time. The vessel had once been a gracious passenger ship but was requisitioned at the outbreak of war. The majority of the crew was drawn from the Royal Naval Reserve, but it is interesting to note twenty-five of them came from the Newfoundland Division. The entire complement of twenty-two officers and 173 men perished. In the days following the tragedy, Irish people had the melancholy sight of many bodies from the *Viknor* being washed ashore. Another local man lost from this ship was Able Seaman Ernest Tidy, aged 17, from 50 High Street, Portslade.

Sergeant Leonard Townsend was a keen footballer and played with Hove Football Club as well as with Brighton & Hove Albion. He and his brother Frederick earned a living by laying down wood paving, but when war was declared they both volunteered in August 1914. Leonard joined the 6/Yorkshire Regiment. He was killed in action in Gallipoli in August 1915, exactly a year after enlisting. His brother, Frederick Charles Townsend, joined *Howe* Battalion, Royal Naval Reserve and became a first class petty officer. He met his death not aboard a ship but in the mud of the Somme where he was part of the 63rd Royal Naval Division. He was killed at Beaumont-Hamel on 12 November 1916. Daisy Moncur wrote to Mr Lister on behalf of the Townsend parents: 'It

First Class Petty Officer Townsend of Howe Battalion was killed in action on the Somme on 12 November 1916. (Hove Library)

was a bitter grief for all of us to lose our dear ones but thank God they were all four men and knew how to die for King and Country and their loved ones at home.'

Another silk postcard sent 'to my dear sister' was adorned appropriately with forget-me-nots. (Author)

Soldiers never forgot their mothers, especially the very young men. It was heart-breaking for those around them when a wounded youngster at the point of death called out for his mother. A great deal of emotion is tied up in this 'to my dear mother'. (Author)

CHAPTER 7

Counting the Cost – The Royal Navy

Britain declared war on 4 August 1914. At Hove there would be no deceptive lull in events with losses being sustained right from the start.

HMS *Pathfinder* was not a relic of the Victorian Navy but a sleek modern cruiser of the Scout class. She could sail at speed and was used for reconnaissance. On 5 September 1914 she was sailing along blithely unaware of the presence of German submarine U-21. A torpedo struck home on the port side near the magazine. HMS *Pathfinder* thus earned the sad distinction of being the first ship sunk by a torpedo fired from a submarine. Out of 268 crew members, 259 were killed, one of them being Able Seaman Arthur Roland Prowse whose parents lived at 23 Tamworth Road, Hove. Prowse was born in London in 1893 and joined the Royal Navy as a boy in 1908. Aboard *Pathfinder* he also had duties as a gun layer.

Just seventeen days later, on 22 September 1914, German submarine U-9 sunk three British armoured cruisers, one after the other, off the Dutch coast. HMS *Aboukir,* HMS *Hogue* and HMS *Cressy* enjoyed a false sense of security because no submarines had been spotted in the area. They maintained an even course without zig-zagging as they were supposed to do and they could not maintain a top speed even if that were desirable. It was also no advantage that the three ships were 14 years old at a time of rapidly changing technology.

When *Aboukir* suffered damage, Captain Drummond, who had been delegated command of the squadron, assumed a mine was to blame and ordered the other two ships to assist. Therefore *Hogue* and *Cressy* stopped to lower their lifeboats. Captain Drummond soon realized he had been the target of a torpedo attack and ordered the other ships away, but it was too late. The three ships sank within the space of an hour-and-a-half. They contained some cadets and many reservists and 1,459 men were killed, amongst them two men from Hove – First Class Petty Officer Harry Hammond from *Hogue* was an experienced sailor aged 40, holder of a Long Service Medal and a Good Conduct Medal and his home address was 15 Suffolk Street where his wife Alice lived, and Second Class Steward Frank Roland Laslett from *Cressy*. Steward Laslett was born at Hove in 1893 and joined the Navy in 1910. He lived at 91 Blatchington Road and was an officers' steward. There were 837 survivors, many plucked from the sea by passing merchant ships.

The subsequent Board of Enquiry laid some blame on Rear Admiral Christian and the captains of the three ships, but it was felt the Admiralty was most at fault for continuing to order old ships to patrol an area of the North Sea called the Broad Fourteens. Some senior officers were firmly against such patrols because they feared the ships were unequal to a challenge from an up-to-date German vessel. Indeed

The Admiralty sanctioned the publication of a series of postcards under the heading 'Britain Prepared' to inform a fascinated public about the Royal Navy. This one was captioned 'British Battleships at sea'. (Author)

Another postcard in the same series was romantically captioned: 'Twilight on the North Sea. The big guns busy.' (Author)

the patrol boats earned the nickname of 'live bait squadron'. It is interesting to note that such patrols were not sent out again. It was also laid down that no major ship should stop for any reason in areas where danger could be present and the necessity of speed and zig-zagging was firmly re-iterated.

On 15 October 1914 this same German vessel U-9 was responsible for the sinking of HMS *Hawke*. The attacks on sister ships HMS *Theseus* and HMS *Hawke* took place off the north-east coast of Scotland. Although they were the oldest vessels on the list of effective ships, they were strongly built with many watertight doors. A torpedo launched against HMS *Theseus* missed its target but the one aimed at HMS *Hawke* struck near the magazine. The result was that the stricken vessel sank within five minutes.

The *Theseus* and *Hawke* were used either for patrol duties or for instructional purposes. This meant there were probably a good many youngsters aboard – cadets or midshipmen in the prime of life. Questions were asked as to whether it was wise to take youngsters aboard warships at a time of hostilities. But it had long been a naval tradition to train boys to work with ships out at sea. Nelson was a midshipman at the age of 12, and Admiral Sir John Fisher, who was so

A torpedo is loaded into the firing tube under the supervision of a rather stiff-looking officer.
(Author)

Here is another postcard from the 'Britain Prepared' series and shows submarine B-6 taking on a torpedo from a supply ship.
(Author)

Submarine B-5 appears to be desperately fragile in this photograph. It was the equivalent of the wood, canvas and wire of the early airplanes. (Author)

Compare the size of submarine B-5 with the huge German submarine U-118, which was launched in 1918 and washed ashore on Hastings beach on 15 April 1919. At the time she was a trophy of war and was being sent to France when the tow-rope broke. (D. Sharp)

passionate about modernising the Navy, was a 14-year-old midshipman when he came under fire aboard HMS *Highflyer.*

The normal full complement of *Hawke* was 544 officers and men but no information was released as to the numbers aboard at the time of the sinking. The naval historian Dan van der Vat states 525 men died. Three local men were lost in *Hawke.* Able Seaman Albert Walter Marler was born at Hove in 1896 and educated at Ellen Street Schools. He enlisted in the Royal Navy on 7 July 1913 and lived at Clarendon Road. Ordinary Seaman Frederick Arthur Jarrold was also born at Hove and was an only child. He was a baker in civilian life and enlisted in the RNVR in March 1913. First Class Boy Ernest Charles Attree was from Portslade and aged only 16 when he died.

Sir John Arbuthnot Fisher modernized the Royal Navy by stepping up training and introducing Dreadnought battleships, as well as the Invincible class of battle cruisers. (Author)

Twenty-one of the crew did survive in an overcrowded boat and were found by a passing Norwegian trawler. They were handed over to the steam trawler *Ben Rinnes* and landed at Aberdeen. It was noted that shortly after the sinking there were other survivors bobbing about on rafts or kept buoyant in the water by their cork lifejackets, but they could not be rescued.

The heavy cruiser HMS *Good Hope* was launched in 1901 and at the outbreak of war was on the reserve list. By the winter of 1914 she was on active service with a largely inexperienced crew, including reservists and cadets. Rear Admiral Sir Christopher Cradock thought she was good enough to become his flagship in the West Indies Squadron whose other members were the heavy cruiser HMS *Monmouth*, the light cruiser HMS *Glasgow* and the converted ex-merchant ship HMS *Otranto*. There was a fifth ship HMS *Canopus*, that failed to join when the others sallied forth to hunt for German ships. The reason given was engine failure but the chief engineer faked it because he was afraid of battle. He was seen by a panel of doctors and despatched back to Britain on board a cargo boat before the battle had even taken place.

The two elderly ships – *Good Hope* and *Monmouth* – together with HMS *Otranto* and the more up-to-date *Glasgow* expected to locate three small cruisers of the Dresden type. An eyewitness aboard the *Otranto* wrote feelingly: 'Imagine our horror when we saw that we had to fight the latest ships of the German Navy, equivalent to our Dreadnoughts.' The ships belonged to the German East Indies Squadron under Admiral Maximilian Graf von Spee and were the *Scharnhorst, Gneisenau, Leipzig* and *Dresden*.

Rear Admiral Sir Christopher Cradock had an impeccable service record and nobody doubted his courage. It would have been no blot on his escutcheon if he had avoided a battle with such a superior force.

HMS Good Hope *was lost with all hands at the battle of Coronel on 1 November 1914.* (Author)

But the recent controversy over the Goeben Affair was on his mind and he had no intention of following Admiral Troubridge's example. What happened was that in the early days of the war Troubridge had made a decision not to chase the German ship *Goeben* in the Mediterranean despite being in command of a large squadron. He was mindful of the order sent by Churchill that no action should be taken against superior forces at that stage and so it was not entirely his fault. Nevertheless there was a Court of Inquiry, followed by a court martial (he was acquitted), but that was the end of his sea-going career.

The German ships manoeuvred themselves into such a position that the British ships were outlined by the setting sun and thus presented a good target. The British ships had plenty of light guns but they were no match for the heavy guns on the *Scharnhorst* and *Gneisenau*. The German ships were thus able to shell them at long range while the British ships could not get close enough for their guns to be effective.

An eyewitness aboard HMS *Otranto* had this to say:

> After being in action for about five minutes [...] the *Good Hope* was on fire about her bridge, and a few minutes later the *Monmouth* was ablaze. The thundering of the guns and the bursting of the shells was now terrible, and if there is a hell of fire it must be a naval battle. At this time we received orders from the *Good Hope* to get out of range of the enemy's guns, which we did. And then all we could do was to look on helpless, and I hope to God in heaven that I will never have to witness such a sight again. There was the *Good Hope* and *Monmouth* on fire and being shelled unmercifully by the enemy, and with over 200 boys on board between them, and 300 men in this ship who could not even raise a hand to help them – only stand and look. At about 7.15 pm a broadside from the enemy hit the *Good Hope* fore of the bridge, and her bows were then almost under water.

Glasgow and *Otranto* obeyed Cradock's orders to make a run for it but *Good Hope* and *Monmouth* sank with all hands, resulting in the death of 1,600 men. It was a tremendous blow to British pride, being her first naval defeat since 1812. This humiliating disaster was known as the Battle of Coronel and was fought off the coast of Chile on 1 November 1914.

Lieutenant French died aboard HMS Good Hope *and this stained glass window once commemorated him at St Andrew's Church, Portslade. Unhappily, it is no longer there.* (Author)

The impressive monument to Lieutenant French is in Portslade Cemetery. (D. Sharp)

In St Andrew's Church, Portslade, there used to be a beautiful stained glass window depicting Jesus walking across the waves to Peter. It was dedicated to the memory of Lieutenant Edward John French aged 31, 'who died in the service of his country in action with a German squadron off the coast of Chili (sic) in which HMS *Good Hope* and HMS *Monmouth* were lost with all hands on board All Saints Day 1914'. This window was removed in recent times when the church was extensively altered to become a community centre and a small chapel. There is also a rose-pink marble memorial with a metal anchor to Lieutenant French in Portslade Cemetery.

Other local men were lost in *Good Hope*. Stoker Harry Avis was born in Piddinghoe in 1883 and later lived at 37 Mortimer Road with his father. A younger brother, Signaller George Avis, born at Barcombe in 1885, was later killed at the Somme and the brothers worked as labourers before joining up. Able Seaman Frederick John Gates was born at Hove on 31 August 1880. He was a postman before the war and lived with his wife at 31 Lennox Road.

Lastly there was Lieutenant Gordon Evelyn Eliott Gray who was born on 19 December 1887 in Assam where his father was deputy commissioner. Like many Indian-born British children, he was despatched home at a tender age for his education. He was around 6 years of age when he came to Hove to live with his grandmother and aunt at 52 Norton Road. He was educated at Windlesham House, Brighton and Bedford Grammar School. In 1902 he went to the training ship HMS *Britannia* and took several first class certificates in naval exams. When he was appointed to the submarine A-4 he was the youngest submarine commander in the Navy. He transferred to the hydro-graphics department and was serving in that capacity in Bermuda when war broke out. There is a handwritten note: 'If I come back I shall have tales to tell, and if not you will know that I have done my duty.'

The Admiralty at once ordered a British squadron to seek out and destroy these German ships. Admiral Frederick Sturdee hurried south from home waters with HMS *Inflexible,* HMS *Invincible* and five light cruisers. They reached Port Stanley, the capital of the Falkland Islands, in early December. HMS *Canopus* was already there, ready to defend the port against any German intrusion.

Meanwhile, Admiral Maximilian Graf von Spee was also headed for the Falklands where he planned to destroy communications and the coaling station. On 8 December 1914 he discovered much to his surprise a British squadron already in residence peacefully replenishing their coal stocks. Indeed they

Lieutenant Gray also died aboard HMS Good Hope *on 1 November 1914.* (Hove Library)

were so engaged in the process and also shrouded in a fog of coal dust, they failed to heed the visual signals from *Canopus*, who then began to fire at *Gneisenau*. The *Gneisenau* and *Nürnberg* quickly departed.

Like Sir Francis Drake finishing his game of bowls before facing the Spanish Armada, Sturdee and his men took around two hours to complete coaling and gear the boilers up to sail at full steam ahead. The British ships quickly overtook the German squadron. Moreover British armament proved superior this time, although the accuracy of the firing was not great at first. The battle cruisers were able to open fire at a distance of 9 miles before the Germans were at the correct distance to sight their guns. Although both British battle cruisers were hit several times, no severe damage was done. Only one man died and five were wounded. By contrast, the *Scharnhorst* capsized taking all her crew with her. The captain of the *Gneisenau* ordered his vessel to be scuttled and the British managed to rescue 176 survivors. Some 2,200 German sailors were lost, including Spee and his two sons who were lieutenants.

Leipzig and *Nürnberg* were also sunk with *Glasgow* taking part in the sinking of *Leipzig*. *Dresden* managed to escape. But *Glasgow* and

This postcard was produced at Southsea and was entitled 'How a British Dreadnought goes into action'. The caption explained that the machinery-loaded guns were capable of dealing out 'destruction at nearly as many miles as the old muzzle-loader was able to do at yards'. (Author)

HMS *Kent* cornered her in March 1915 at Cumberland Bay in an island off Chile. After scuttling their ship the German sailors scrambled ashore. As men aboard *Glasgow* watched *Leipzig* disappear beneath the waves, a petty officer noticed a pig swimming furiously in the water. The animal was badly frightened and nearly succeeded in drowning its kind rescuer. But eventually the pig was taken aboard *Glasgow* and adopted as the ship's mascot where it remained for a year. It was given the name of Tirpitz.

Dreadful as the casualties were in the Battle of Coronel, at least men died under battle conditions. Far worse for the families concerned was the loss of lives in needless accidents. On 26 November 1914 HMS *Bulwark* was moored in the River Medway at a place called Kethole Reach. It was a peaceful early morning scene with men on board eating breakfast when, without any warning, there was a massive explosion. There was extensive damage in Sheerness and the bang was loud enough to rattle Southend Pier. Churchill was obliged to tell the House of Commons that 700 men had been killed and there were just twelve survivors. Naturally enough, thoughts turned to sabotage but the most likely explanation was that something went wrong as ammunition was being taken on board.

Six months later there was a similar accident on 27 May 1915. This time the blame was laid squarely on defective mine charges and HMS *Princess Irene* was moored on the River Medway at Sheerness Harbour to await replacements. The explosion was so fierce that debris and body parts rained down on adjacent villages. The number of dead was put at 278 and they were not all Navy personnel either because seventy-eight were local workers.

Two Hove casualties from *Bulwark* were youngsters. They were First Class Boy Sydney Victor Moore, who was born at Hove in 1897, educated at Portland Road Schools and joined the Navy in 1912. He lived at 71 Goldstone Villas. First Class Boy John Alexander Fay Reid was born in Gibraltar and worked as a messenger before enlisting on 14 January 1913. His parents lived at 16 Conway Place. The

First Class Boy John Alexander Reid died aboard HMS Bulwark on 26 November 1914.
(Hove Library)

casualty from *Princess Irene* was First Class Torpedo-man Albert Victor Butland, who was born at Hove in 1893 and educated at George Street Schools. He lived at 33 Belfast Street. He joined the Royal Navy as a boy on 6 February 1911 and trained on HMS *Ganges II.*

Between the Mediterranean and the Sea of Marmara is an area known as the Dardanelles. The Turks blocked this passage to Britain and her allies and their ships could not enter the Black Sea and neither could Russia export or import goods as usual. There was a stalemate on the Western Front and Russia wanted some sort of diversion to reduce pressure on her troops. Thus a plan was formed for a demonstration or show of arms involving the British Navy in the Dardanelles. This escalated into an attack on the many forts lining the shores of the Dardanelles and in turn led to the disastrous Gallipoli landings.

Many people lay the blame for the debacle squarely at the door of Winston Churchill and indeed his reputation suffered to such an extent that it was a wonder he ever rose to prominence again. But the situation was complex and there were other men who were found wanting too. Probably the fact that three outstanding personalities with opposing views were involved did not help matters. There was Admiral Fisher with his vast naval experience, and he did not speak out when he should have done. Field Marshal Kitchener stubbornly refused at first to allow any troops to be sent to the Dardanelles, whereas a combined operation from the start offered the only possibility of success. Churchill was over-optimistic about the prowess of the British Navy. The War Council never questioned Kitchener's advice nor sought opinions from naval experts, and the council did not even meet when hostilities were actually taking place. The British badly underestimated the Turkish forces, which had the benefit of German advice and expertise and failed to recognize the dangers of the extensive minefields laid by German submarines and, indeed, possible attacks from the submarines themselves.

Nelson once said: 'Any sailor who attacks a fort is a fool.' The Navy knew the value of this advice, which was still sound in the twentieth century. But Churchill ignored it and the shelling of the forts by ships of the Royal Navy commenced on 19 February 1915. Accuracy was essential but this was not forthcoming. There was the distance, the choppy waters and British naval guns did not have the right elevation

This type of aircraft operated as a naval scout in 1916. It sought out enemy positions and also reported on the fall of shot from British battleships to make shelling more accurate. (Author)

to succeed. Aircraft were needed to go up and estimate the fall of shot but this was not always possible. Meanwhile, the mobile Howitzer batteries on shore were causing serious damage. By March 1915 it was clear the British ships were not having the expected impact and orders were given for a withdrawal.

HMS *Inflexible* arrived at the Dardanelles on 24 January 1915 and some three weeks later she started to bombard Turkish forts, but

Alfred Wilfrid Blaker of HMS Inflexible *died at the Dardanelles on 9 March 1915. His mother donated the oak reredos at St Nicolas Church, Portslade, in his memory.* (D. Sharp)

without much success. A few weeks later she was busy firing her guns on the 15 and 18 March trying to silence Turkish ordnance and give British minesweepers a better chance of success. But *Inflexible* struck a mine and was hit a number of times.

On 18 March 1915, Lieutenant Arthur Wilfrid Blaker of HMS *Inflexible* was killed in action and buried at sea. He was born on 27 March 1889 and came from a notable Portslade family. He was the son of Arthur Beckett Blaker, who married his second cousin Elizabeth Jane. Her father was Edward Blaker of Easthill House, Portslade, and he was twice married, each wife producing six children. The young lieutenant's mother had become a widow in 1914 and now had lost her eldest son. In his memory she donated the oak reredos in St Nicolas Church, Portslade, which is still in place to this day.

Also caught up in the bombardment of Turkish forts was HMS *Majestic*, who opened fire on 18 March. *Majestic's* target was Fort 9, but unbeknown to the captain, Turkish field guns were cleverly screened in adjoining woodland. The vessel sustained four direct hits resulting in one death while some men were wounded. But *Majestic* was not badly damaged and four days later was back on duty. On 27 May 1915, German submarine U-21 torpedoed *Majestic* at Cape Helles causing her to capsize within nine minutes and the loss of forty-nine lives. It was the same submarine U-21 that had sunk HMS *Pathfinder* in 1914. The Hove casualty was Stoker Frederick Upward, who was educated at George Street Schools and later lived with his wife at 8 Victoria Cottages, right on Hove's sea-front.

Before the war HMS *Newmarket*, built in 1907, was a civilian ship carrying passengers or cargo. During the war she became an auxiliary minesweeper and served at the Dardanelles. On 17 July 1917 German submarine UC-38 torpedoed her in the Aegean Sea, south of Nikaria Island. She sank with the loss of seventy lives, including Ordinary Seaman Sydney Benton, who was educated at Hove High School in Clarendon Villas. His father, Arthur Benton of 208 Church Road, wrote to the Admiralty for news of his son and received the following reply dated 20 August 1917:

I have to state for your information that HMS *Newmarket* sailed from Port Laki, in the Aegean Sea, on the 16th ultimo, to go to the assistance of a vessel attacked by an enemy submarine.

Nothing further has been heard of the ship, and despite a most exhaustive search of the whole neighbourhood, no trace has been found of her or her crew. In these circumstances, it is deeply regretted that all on board must, it is feared, now be definitely regarded as having lost their lives.

Ordinary Seaman Sydney Benton was lost aboard HMS Newmarket. (Hove Library)

The landings at Gallipoli involved fierce fighting and eventual evacuation. The first British troops landed there on 25 April 1915 while ANZAC units landed in the wrong place. In fact the latter were in such a tight spot that four battalions of the Royal Naval Reserve were despatched as reinforcements. It was Churchill's idea to form the 63rd Royal Naval Division, composed mostly of reservists who were not needed at sea, although there were some marines. The four battalions were the 1st (*Drake*), the 5th (*Nelson*), the 6th (*Howe*) and the 7th (*Hood*).

HMS Queen Elizabeth *was the most modern of the British battleships to take part in the Dardanelles campaign. She served as flagship in the preliminary battle and again at Gallipoli but was far too valuable to risk in the forefront of battle.* (Author)

The local men who died were as follows:

Drake Battalion
Leading Seaman George Sowter

Nelson Battalion
Able Seaman Joseph Card

Howe Battalion
Sub-Lieutenant Ernest Alfred Clifford
Able Seaman Herbert Henry Jestico
Sub-Lieutenant Joseph Sandbach
First Class Petty Officer Frederick Charles Townsend

Able Seaman Card lived at 51 Coleridge Street and joined the Royal Navy on 18 August 1914.

Sub-Lieutenant Clifford was born at Datchet in 1874. He joined the Royal Navy as a boy on 3 April 1889 but by 1914 was living at 3 Coastguard Cottages, Hove, where he was the naval instructor in gunnery at the local RNVR base. He was killed in action on 4 June 1915. His widow received a letter from Sub-Lieutenant Joseph Sandbach, who was to be killed six weeks later. He wrote that Sub-Lieutenant Clifford died in action: 'leading his men in as gallant a charge against the Turks, as was ever known in history; out of 118 men who he was leading only twenty-five returned.' Lieutenant Colonel Charles Collins, commander of *Howe* Battalion, also wrote a letter when he arrived back in England:

> As soon as we heard we were going to leave the Peninsular, we prepared a strong cross of hard wood, covered it with brass from empty shell cases and had it erected close to the spot where your husband lost his life […] The consecration service took place in the night before we left and was very impressive. A quarter moon was shining, and to our right lay the sea, which he loved so well, lit up persistently by the Turkish searchlights from the Dardanelles, whilst over us an artillery duel raged unceasingly […] all of us felt terribly sad at leaving this ground, which we had so hardly won and which had cost

us so many precious lives. Of all those left behind I doubt if there was one who did his duty so gallantly and conscientiously as your husband [...] his example will ever be an inspiration to those who knew him of how an Englishman should behave.

Sub-Lieutenant Sandbach was born in 1876 and joined the Navy as a boy in 1891. He lived for some years at Hove Coastguard Station and was instructor to Number 2 Company (Brighton & Hove) Sussex Division RNVR. After his death in action on 20 July 1915, Lieutenant Commander Isger wrote:

Poor old Sandbach [...] he has been my comrade clean through, first as chief petty officer and then as sub-lieutenant and a finer chap and comrade you could not meet. The day before [he was killed] he assisted me in carrying out a plan of mine [...] It meant crawling through a hole into the Turks' trench, and finding out if they were there; had they been there it would have meant certain death. We found, however, that those who could do so had fled, and that the Turkish trenches were a solid mass of dead. The result of our reconnaissance was that we took all points that it had been desired to capture and 150 yards beyond.' Sandbach was shot 'practically in the hour of victory and glory'.

Gunner John Henry Day was born in Hull but when war broke out he was living at 1 Clarendon Villas and was a dentistry apprentice. He joined the RNVR in August 1914 as a bugler. When he was 18 he was sent out to assist in the relief of Antwerp and returned home safely. On 1 March 1915 he left for Gallipoli in *Howe* Battalion and fought in the trenches for the whole of the campaign. He was killed on 2 August 1917 while serving his gun on the SS *Newlyn*.

Able Seaman Jestico was born in Hove in 1897 and before the war he was a clerk at the Goldstone Bakery in Fonthill Road. He joined the Navy in 1914 but was killed on 21 May 1915. His parents, Isaac and Annie Jestico, lived at 132 Ellen Street and his brother, Sergeant Francis William Jestico, was killed in action at Ypres.

Second Lieutenant Walter Gerard Paling was born at 31 Clarendon

Villas in 1890 and educated at Hove High School. He was a clerk at Barclays Bank's head office in North Street, Brighton, and lived at 2 Hartington Villas, Hove. He enlisted as an Able Seaman in *Howe* Battalion in August 1914 and was Mentioned in Despatches by General Sir Charles Munro because he 'behaved in a gallant and courageous manner in action from 18 August to 24 December at Cape Helles'. Afterwards he served in France and in 1917 was promoted and placed in the Special Reserve of Officers and attached to the 3/Royal Sussex. He survived the war.

Private Sydney Theodore Sang was a Cadet in the RNVR in 1914 and the following year was sent to the Dardanelles with *Howe* Battalion under Major Kenneth Ford. He spent his 15th birthday in the trenches at Gallipoli. He returned home in 1916 and his parents wished him to complete his education, but after a short time he left to join the Liverpool Scottish as a bugler and then transferred to the Scottish Rifles. He was killed in action in France on 2 September 1918 at the age of 18.

Local soldiers who died at Gallipoli were as follows:

Lieutenant Raymond de Lusignan, Royal Dublin Fusiliers
Lieutenant George Leonard Cheesman, Hampshire Regiment
Captain Robert Cecil Colville Frankland, South Staffordshire Regiment
Brigadier Major Thomas Hugh Colville Frankland, Royal Dublin Fusiliers
Corporal Frederic Lane, City of London Yeomanry
Private Clement Henry Matthews, Royal Sussex Regiment
Private Sidney Wigmore Shaw, Australian Imperial Force
Trooper Reginald Douglas Warren, Royal East Kent Regiment
Private Walter Williams, Royal Munster Fusiliers

Lieutenant Cheesman was an educated man having been to university and earned his M.A. degree. He was killed in action in Suvla Bay on 11 May 1915.

Trooper Harold Colbourne was born at Willesden Green in 1897. He was educated at Hove High School and enlisted in the Sussex Yeomanry in November 1914 while still a schoolboy. He was sent to Gallipoli where he contracted dysentery and was invalided back to

England. He died of pleural pneumonia at home 12 Raphael Road on 12 May 1916.

The Frankland brothers were sons of Colonel Colville Frankland and his wife Mary, who lived at 67 Brunswick Place, although the brothers were both living at Eastbourne at the outbreak of war. Brigadier Major T.H.C. Frankland was born in Cork on 17 October 1879 and was educated at Charterhouse and Sandhurst. In 1899 he joined the 2/Royal Dublin Fusiliers and saw action in South Africa, being awarded the relevant medal. He was killed in action on the very first day of operations at Gallipoli on 25 April but not before he had ensured his men took the safest way up the cliffs. During this action he took a rifle from a fallen soldier and shot four Turkish soldiers himself at a range of 20 to 30 yards. Captain Farmer of the Headquarters Staff, 29th Division, wrote to his family: 'I attribute the success of the landing and progress on the first day largely to Frankland's bravery, skill and example. He gave the right lead.'

Winston Churchill also wrote a letter:

I am very much indebted to you for sending me an account of my cherished and gallant friend's death. It was a sorrow in these sad times to me to learn that he had fallen. We had always kept in touch with one another since the armoured train fight in Natal in 1899. He was every inch a soldier, and in him the army and the country loses an officer of high ability and absolute self-devotion [...] I should be glad if you would endeavour to procure me a photograph of Tom, preferably in his uniform.

The Boers captured both Churchill and Frankland and kept them as prisoners of war in the States Model Schools where they shared a dormitory. Churchill encouraged Frankland to draw coloured campaign maps so that they could keep abreast of the Boer War as and when they could glean information. Frankland does not seem to have harboured any resentment when Churchill managed to escape leaving him to languish as a prisoner. But perhaps it was on Churchill's conscience because six months later at the camp to which they had been moved, Frankland was astonished to see two khaki-clad figures galloping furiously towards them. It was Churchill and his cousin the Duke of Marlborough, who had outstripped the advancing British Army to tell him he was a free man.

Frankland's brother, Captain R.C.C. Frankland, was born in County Wicklow on 7 July 1877; he too went to Charterhouse. He was also a Boer War veteran and settled in South Africa where he divided his time between army service and a post in the South African Civil Service. But as soon as he heard war had broken out, he left and came home to fight for his country, joining the South Staffordshire Regiment. He was killed in action at Suvla Bay on 8 August 1915.

Walter Heather was born at Hove in 1889 and lived in Church Road with his wife. He was a schoolmaster at East Hove Schools and joined the Sussex Yeomanry in 1910, being mobilized in August 1914. He was attached to the Royal Field Artillery and served throughout the Gallipoli campaign. He served two years in France and in June 1917 was sent home from Egypt to be commissioned as a second lieutenant. He was awarded the Belgian Croix de Guerre and survived the war. In September 1919 he resumed his teaching career.

Corporal Lane was born at London in 1882. By 1914 he lived in Langdale Road and was an employee of the Car & General Insurance Company of London. He served six years in the Territorial Force before war broke out and later joined the City of London Yeomanry (Roughriders). He was killed in action on 29 October 1915 aged 33 and buried at the foot of Chocolate Hill, Suvla Bay. His commanding officer wrote: 'He has done his duty throughout, like a man, facing all dangers, without flinching.'

Second Lieutenant Thomas Frederick Oliver was born in Bristol and educated at Harrow but later lived with his widowed mother at 26 Brunswick Terrace. He was a civil engineer before enlisting in September 1914, originally in the Public Schools Battalion, then in the 12/Sherwood Foresters and temporarily in the 13th Battalion. He was wounded in action at Gallipoli and from December 1916 served in France but was invalided out on 24 February 1917. He died at home on 26 October 1916 from heart failure following pneumonia.

Trooper Thomas Page was born in Hastings in 1887. When war broke out he had been living in Dunedin, New Zealand for six months but he immediately enlisted in the 7/Mounted Otago Rifles. He was wounded at Gallipoli on 14 August 1915 and died on 20 September

1915. He was buried at Hove Cemetery because his parents lived at 61 Tamworth Road.

Corporal Albert Walter Paish was born in Hove in 1880. He already had a taste of military life as he held the South African Medal but by 1914 he had been living in Australia for around two years. He enlisted in the Australian Imperial Yeomanry and was wounded at Gallipoli. He died at Malta on 10 July 1915.

Lieutenant Frederick Parsons was born at Hove in 1890 and was the son of Fred Parsons, the well-known Hove builder with business premises at Church Road. His parents lived at 6 Sackville Road. Fred sent his sons to be educated at Steyning Grammar School. When he grew up Frederick went to Australia where he took up farming. At the outbreak of war he joined the 1st Australian Division. He landed at Gallipoli on 25 April 1915 and was there for the whole of the campaign. He was shot through the arm but recovered. Afterwards he served in Egypt and then in France. In April 1917 he received the Military Medal from the hands of General Birdwood in France. Meanwhile, Captain Robert Henderson Parsons, his brother, was also serving in the Army, having first been commissioned to the Territorial Force in 1910. He was awarded the Military Cross in 1918. Both brothers survived the war.

Trooper Shaw was once a member of the Sussex Yeomanry but in 1909 he emigrated to Australia and when war was declared he joined the Australian Imperial Force. He became part of the ANZAC troops at Gallipoli but was killed in action on 11 May 1915.

Private Frank Henry Vickers was born at Brighton in 1889. He became an estate agent and lived at 4 Gwydyr Mansions. In September 1914 he enlisted in the 1/Field Company Engineers New Zealand Expeditionary Force. He was at Gallipoli when he fell ill with typhoid and was taken to Malta where he died on 25 August 1915.

Trooper Warren had once been a clerk in Lloyd's Bank in Hove. He was part of the South Eastern Mounted Brigade and was killed in action at Gallipoli on 7 December 1915. He was aged 20.

Private Williams was a Portslade man. He previously served with the Lancers but when he was killed in action on 21 August 1915 he was with the Royal Munster Rifles.

When it became obvious that the Gallipoli campaign could not succeed, the troops and their supplies were quietly withdrawn. This turned out to be the most brilliant action of the whole expedition because it was carried out with such expertise that the Turks did not suspect a thing and not a man was lost.

On Boxing Day 1915, Submarine E-6 was ordered out from Harwich to patrol an area of the North Sea near the Horn Reefs to search for enemy submarines. As she approached the reefs E-6 should have been on high alert because an armed trawler, *Resono*, had recently struck a mine in the area. Perhaps the captain was unaware of this incident but a passing torpedo boat sent E-6 a signal warning of the danger. It seems that although the message was received, it was not properly evaluated because she did not alter course. She struck a mine and sank with all hands including Lieutenant Alfred Gledhill, who was born at Hove in 1889. 'Many residents of Brighton and Hove will learn with regret that Lieutenant Alfred Gledhill [...] met his death while in the execution of his duty on 26 December last. He will be remembered by many as a chorister in the old parish church, Hove, and also an old Connaught Road schoolboy.'[5]

When war broke out he was serving as Fourth Officer aboard a White Star Line vessel but at once offered his services to his country. At first he was engaged on transport duties and was sent to Australia to embark the first contingent of troops from that country. Then he went on patrol duty in the North Sea, 'where his sterling seamanship earned him the esteem of his superior officers and crew who on his promotion to navigating lieutenant on another ship presented him with an inscribed gold watch.'[5] His mother remarried and became Mrs Chambers of 24 Portland Road.

The Battle of Jutland was fought on 31 May/1 June 1916. It involved the British Grand Fleet under Admiral Jellicoe and a battle cruiser squadron under Admiral Beatty against the German High Seas Fleet under Admiral Scheer, and a separate group of battle cruisers under Admiral Hipper. The first ships to engage were the battle cruisers but both sides were unaware that their enemy's main fleet was a short distance away.

The battle was a complicated one with heroism and mistakes on both sides. The British fielded a smaller number of ships to the Germans with the numbers being twenty-one vessels to thirty-seven. The outcome was inconclusive in terms of outright victory or defeat but it is true to state that had Germany won a complete victory, it is more than likely they would have gone on to win the war. When the German fleet returned home they were treated to a heroes' welcome and the public celebrated a historic victory, while in Britain there was gloom with flags flying at half-mast.

On paper the figures look bleak for the British who lost eight destroyers, three battle cruisers and three armoured cruisers. Around 6,097 men were killed, 510 were wounded and 177 were picked up by the Germans and became prisoners of war. The Germans lost one battle cruiser, one armoured cruiser, four light cruisers and five torpedo boats, while 2,551 men died.

The outcome of the battle of Jutland was by no means clear-cut. Indeed a rumour circulated that Admiral Jellicoe had been court-marshalled and shot for 'losing' the battle. (Author)

The ships seen at anchor off Hove in July 1914 were involved in the Battle of Jutland. HMS *Marlborough* fired 162 shells but a torpedo found its target and two crewmen were killed and two were wounded. The ship also developed a slight list and after the battle needed to be towed back to harbour for repairs. HMS *Colossus* also came under fire and was hit twice, but only suffered minor damage while nine men were wounded. By 1916 HMS *Hercules* had transferred to the 4th Battle Squadron where she served as the flagship. In 1915 HMS *Superb* had joined the 4th Battle Squadron, followed the next year by HMS *St Vincent* and HMS *Vanguard.* All these ships survived Jutland.

HMS *Invincible* was Admiral Hood's flagship of the 3rd Battle Cruiser Squadron. She was a massive ship of 17,250 tons and boasted a battery of eight 12-inch guns. She was able to make a fast speed of 26 knots because she was unhindered by the weight of protective armour. Unfortunately, at the Battle of Jutland when she was under heavy fire, a shot found its way down 'Q' turret, causing the magazine to explode and the ship to sink. Indeed the explosion was so fierce the ship broke into three parts – her mid-ship sinking to the ocean floor while her up-ended bows and stern were still visible on the surface. Some 1,025 officers and men were killed including Admiral Hood. The *Badger* picked up six survivors.

Local men from *Invincible* killed at Jutland were as follows:

Leading Signalman Ernest George Aldous
Carpenter Henry Marshall Arthur Patching
Chief Engine-Room Artificer Robert Darney Ramsay
Chief Stoker Arthur Corney from Portslade

Leading Signalman Aldous was a shop porter before joining the Navy in 1904 as a boy. He went to the training ship *St Vincent* and from 1904 to 1905 was aboard HMS *Terrible* on a tour to India. He also saw service at the battle off Heligoland and at the Falklands. His parents lived at 114 Montgomery Street.

Carpenter Patching was born at Hove in 1895 and was educated at Ellen Street Schools. He lived at 9 Linton Road and his parents lived at 83 Payne Avenue. His brother, Private Richard George Patching, a motor mechanic, joined the 13/Royal Sussex and was killed in action at Richebourg on 30 June 1916. Their father Henry Marshall Patching, followed an army career in the Durham Light Infantry for seventeen years and served another three years in the Great War, but survived unscathed.

Chief Engine-Room Artificer Robert Darney Ramsay was born at Aberdour, Fife, in 1882 but later settled in Hove where he lived at 67 Errol Road. He joined the Royal Navy in 1904. He also saw service aboard *Invincible* at the Battle of the Falklands.

HMS *Queen Mary* was a modern battle cruiser and she was the last to be launched by the Royal Navy before hostilities began. At Jutland she put up a splendid fight but the German vessels *Seydlitz* and *Derfflinger* targeted her. When she was hit amidships, she exploded, sending debris high into the air, which then rained down in charred bits and pieces over two adjacent British ships. The death toll of the ship's company came to 1,200 officers and men, with two officers and five men wounded. A German ship picked up one officer and one man.

Local men from *Queen Mary* who died were as follows:

Fourth Class Engine-Room Artificer George Henry Blackman
Acting Leading Stoker Richard Harry How
Leading Stoker Ernest Lightfoot
First Class Stoker Albert Bertie Colbourne

Engine-Room Artificer Blackman was educated at Greenwich School but little is known about his life because his aunt, who lived at 21 Stoneham Road, filled in his service card with the barest of details. His father used to live at Hove but moved to Penge.

First Class Stoker Colbourne was aged 22 when he died. His parents lived at 9 East Street, Portslade.

Acting Leading Stoker How was born at Plumstead on 2 January 1894. He was educated at East Hove Schools and lived at 7 Ruskin Road. Before enlisting, he was a grocer's assistant.

Leading Stoker Lightfoot was born at Hove on 14 August 1891. He was a married man whose wife lived in Goldstone Road. He was a professional sailor but there is no date of enlistment given on his record card.

The battle cruiser HMS *Lion* was launched in 1910 and at Jutland she was Admiral Beatty's flagship. She might have perished because of a serious fire aboard but the courageous turret commander gave orders to flood the magazine and thus the ship was saved. He died in the action and was later awarded a Victoria Cross. It is interesting to note that the crew included an alert sailor from Hove. He was Gunner Arthur Atkinson, who was subsequently awarded £5 for sighting and sinking an enemy submarine.

The fate of HMS *Ardent* was particularly tragic. She was a member of the 4th Destroyer Flotilla and survived the Battle of Jutland without much damage. She then found herself alone and unsure of the position of the rest of her division but unbeknown to her officers, that division had ceased to exist. The *Ardent* sailed south and when smoke was spotted ahead sailed towards it. But the smoke was issuing from a German ship and *Ardent* did not hesitate to attack at once. The crew were unable to see ahead because the searchlights of four battleships dazzled their eyes. The German Dreadnought *Westfalen* delivered the fatal shot, then the warships turned off their lights and sailed away leaving the crew to die in utter blackness. Lieutenant Commander Marsden and one crewman were the only two men to survive. At the top of the official list of the seventy-seven men who died was Lieutenant Edward Francis Egan. He was educated at Marlborough House School in The Drive, Hove and his name is recorded on the school's memorial tablet in All Saints Church, Hove, although it does not appear on Hove's Roll of Honour.

HMS *Hampshire* was also present at the Battle of Jutland. She could be classed as an elderly armoured cruiser because she was launched in 1903. But she returned to base at Scapa Flow safely on 3 June 1916. Two days later she sailed on an important mission transporting Lord Kitchener, the war minister, to Archangel in order to hold a meeting with Tsar Nicholas II of Russia to explain the British role in the war, both in terms of military action and the all-important financial situation.

The voyage must have been deemed too important to postpone although conditions at sea were dreadful and fierce gales continued unabated. The *Hampshire* had only been tossed about for one hour before Captain Savill took the decision to head back home. Unhappily, the ship sailed straight into a minefield of twenty-two devices planted by German submarine U-75 a few nights previously. The *Hampshire* exploded between the Brough of Birsay and Warwick Head and sank quite quickly. The shore was only one-and-a-half miles away and there should have been more survivors. But in the stormy conditions lifeboats either became snagged in the rigging or were

The formidable Lord Horatio Herbert Kitchener was not much given to smiling. This postcard was captioned triumphantly 'Lord Kitchener smiles'. He was lost aboard HMS Hampshire *on 5 June 1916.* (Author)

smashed against the ship. Many sailors died of exposure rather than from injuries sustained in the explosion. Fourteen men managed to reach the shore but two of them died before rescue arrived. When news of the disaster reached the authorities no less than four ships of the Grand Fleet were hurriedly despatched to search for survivors, followed by five other ships, but when they arrived at the scene there was nothing to see apart from the boiling sea. Some of the survivors said that Kitchener was still alive after the explosion because they were ordered to make way for him. But nobody knows what happened after that.

Two Hove men were lost from *Hampshire*. Lieutenant Benjamin Pelham Knowle Greenhill was born at Knowle Hall, Bridgwater, Somerset in 1881. He lived at 18 Seafield Road with his wife but did not need to earn a living since he had private means. He was already in the RNVR before he joined the Royal Navy on 4 August 1914 as a sub-lieutenant. After his death his widow removed herself from the proximity of the sea and went to live at 51 Highdown Road.

First Class Stoker Alexander Douglas Stringer also died. He was born at Hove on 25 August 1893 and educated at Ellen Street Schools. He lived with his parents at 73 Tamworth Road and later earned a living as a sawyer and box-maker. He joined the Royal Navy on 21 April 1913.

The destroyer HMS *Opal* was present at the Battle of Jutland and although she attacked some German ships and was fired upon in return, she survived the conflict. However, in a battle of a different sort she was not so successful. On 12 January 1918 she set forth on a Dark Night Patrol to search for any German vessels that might be laying mines.

First Class Stoker Alexander Douglas Stringer was also lost aboard HMS Hampshire.
(Hove Library)

She was in the company of her sister ship HMS *Narborough* and the light cruiser HMS *Boadicea*. The weather conditions were fine at first but then a fierce blizzard blew in, the waves increased in height and there was no visibility at all. The two destroyers were in danger of foundering and the captain of the *Boadicea* ordered them back to Scapa Flow. They sailed slowly homewards but four hours later the *Boadicea* received a message from *Opal* to say she had run aground. The weather conditions were so atrocious that no ships could be sent to search and it was two days later that the two battered wrecks were discovered with no life aboard either of them.

The memorial at Windwick Bay, South Ronaldsay, reads: 'In memory of the 188 men who perished here when HMS *Narborough* and HMS *Opal* were lost on the rocks of Hesta during the snowstorm of 12 January 1918.' A victim from *Opal* was Ordinary Seaman Frederick William Tubbs Holdstock. He was born in Portslade in

Ordinary Seaman Holdstock of HMS Opal *died on 12 January 1918.* (Hove Library)

1899 and later lived at 30 Linton Road, Hove. He worked as a laundry hand before joining up on 8 March 1917. Two brothers were killed while serving with the Army.

There was only one survivor and he was Able Seaman William Sissons from the *Opal*. He was able to tell the Board of Enquiry about events leading up to the tragedy. He said when *Opal* ran aground first, she gave three blasts on her siren to warn *Narborough* and she replied. But in trying to turn she keeled over and was lost too. Boats, whalers and carley crafts were launched but the sea overwhelmed them. Sissons clung onto the mid-ship funnel, watching for his chance and then swam to the shore. He found shelter in a small cave and on 14 January managed to attract the attention of a trawler by waving an ensign that had washed up on the shore.

On 24 March 1916 the captain of German submarine UB-29 made a mistake. He thought the ship he was observing was a British minelayer and consequently a torpedo was fired. But the vessel was the ferry *Sussex* peacefully engaged in taking passengers across the English Channel. The explosion tore off part of the ship and caused the death of fifty passengers. The rest of the ferry stayed afloat and eventually a trawler arrived on the scene and towed her into Boulogne. The incident caused consternation in the United States because although there were no American civilians killed, some twenty-five were injured. On 19 April 1916 President Woodrow Wilson threatened to break off diplomatic relations with Germany. At first Germany denied responsibility but then decided it would not be a good idea to provoke the United States into entering the war and thus on 6 May 1916 the Sussex Pledge came about. Germany promised not to target passenger ships or unarmed merchant ships.

The Sussex Pledge did not even last a year. In the early months of 1917 the German Naval Command decided to take a gamble on bringing Britain to its knees within five months by means of submarine warfare with no holds barred. Since Britain was so reliant on imports of food and raw materials, it seemed a safe bet. Indeed a gloomy Admiral Jellicoe thought supplies might run out by July. Not surprisingly neutral merchant ships refused to leave port and in April 1917 British shipping losses climbed to 875,000 tons. Prime Minister Lloyd George insisted that a convoy system must be instituted at once and this came about on 10 May 1917. The situation was so desperate it had to be done despite the grave reservations of the Admiralty. Neither was Admiral Beatty happy at having so many light cruisers detached from his precious Grand Fleet to mount anti-submarine search-and-destroy missions.

The Zeebrugge Raid originated in the audacious brain of Admiral Sir Roger Keyes. The popular view of the 1918 event is that it was a gung-ho expedition, expensive in the loss of personnel and ultimately unsuccessful – in short, one of those glorious but futile British actions. This perception needs to be challenged. Zeebrugge veterans were less than enchanted by British historians' official accounts, especially as it appeared they favoured the German version of events, which naturally minimized the impact. But the raid was meticulously planned, innovative measures were adopted and it did achieve its objective.

The reason for the Zeebrugge Raid was that since 1914 the Germans had turned this small stretch of Belgian coast into a naval and military powerhouse. Although today we associate picturesque Bruges with quaint houses and tranquil waterways, during the Great War it was important for the facilities of its dockyards. Here German submarines could be repaired quickly and without the time and expense involved in returning to a base in Germany.

In this view of Zeebrugge the extraordinary length of the mole can be appreciated. The monument commemorates the British raid on 23 April 1918.
(Author)

The entrance to the Bruges canal was shielded by the enormous mole at Zeebrugge stretching for over one-and-a-half miles, describing a graceful arc to the north-east. It is the longest mole in the world. Nor was the mole a stumpy edifice but loomed to a height of 29 feet. The parapet itself was 3 feet higher than the interior footway and then there was a further drop of around 16 feet onto the main causeway. The mole was joined to the shore by a viaduct. At the time of the raid an 8-knot current swirled along the mole and there was a terrific swell.

Although the Germans must have thought nobody would be foolish enough to attack such a strong position, they left nothing to chance. There was the full panoply of wartime defence measures including blockhouses, barbed wire, heavy guns, machine-guns, anti-aircraft guns, plus a 1,000-strong garrison.

The British plan was that three aged naval vessels filled with cement would be sunk in the Bruges canal, thus making it impassable. But in order for the block-ships *Thetis, Intrepid* and *Iphigenia* to manoeuvre into position, a diversion was planned in the shape of an attack on the mole. To prevent reinforcements pouring onto the mole an obsolete British submarine C-3 containing a deadly cargo of explosives was wedged under the viaduct and blown up.

Lieutenant Richard Sandford was in charge of C-3 and he was awarded a Victoria Cross for his brave actions, one of eight VCs won in the raid. It is pleasant to record that when Lieutenant Richard Sandford and his crew had to abandon ship, his brother Captain Francis Sandford sailed to the rescue in a picket boat. The brothers were sons of the Venerable E.G. Sandford, Archdeacon of Exeter, and there were three other brothers, all successful men, including one who was an English rugby international.

The monument subsequently erected on the mole at Zeebrugge bears the following inscription:

Here under close fire from the parapet
The submarine C-3, filled with explosive
Was driven into the pile work of the mole
And blew a complete breach 150 feet long

C-3 was accompanied by fellow submarine C-1, but unfortunately the towrope broke and she arrived at the scene of action too late to be of any use.

Pen & Sword Books

FREEPOST SF5

47 Church Street

BARNSLEY

South Yorkshire

S70 2BR

DISCOVER MORE ABOUT HISTORY

Pen & Sword Books now offer over 3,000 titles in print covering all aspects of history including Military, Maritime, Aviation, Local, Family, Transport, Crime, Political and soon Social History. We also do books on nostalgia and have now introduced a range of military DVD's and Historical Fiction. If you would like to receive our catalogues and leaflets on new books and offers, please fill in the details below and return this card (no postage required).

Alternatively, register online at www.pen-and-sword.co.uk.

(Please note: we do not sell data information to any third party companies).

Visit www.WarfareMagazine.co.uk for free military history content including commemorative anniversary articles, military news, reviews, competitions and new product releases.

Title .... Name...

Address...

.... Postcode..............................

Email Address ....

If you wish to receive our email newsletter, please tick here

Website: www.pen-and-sword.co.uk • Email: enquiries@pen-and-sword.co.uk
Telephone: 01226 734222 • Fax: 01226 734438

The memorial at Zeebrugge recalls the heroic action of submarine C-3 on St George's Day 1918 and the men who took part. (Author)

The men who took part in the Zeebrugge Raid were all volunteers: married men or men with family commitments were weeded out. The men were also given two or three chances to opt out without dishonour and they knew it was a dangerous mission. Perhaps the most nerve-wracking part was waiting around for the action to begin. Twice they psyched themselves up for the worst, the requisite tot of rum was issued, and twice the raid was cancelled – once when the ships were nearing Zeebrugge and the second time after only an hour at sea but weather conditions had to be just right. Then there was a wait of ten days for the appropriate tide. The raid finally happened on the eve and day of St George's Day, 22/23 April 1918. Some 1,700 men took part and the astonishing number of seventy-eight craft were involved from sixteen coastal motor boats to seventeen destroyers, the monitors *Erebus* and *Terror*, plus Admiral Keynes' flagship HMS *Warwick*.

Iris was an erstwhile ferry working on the Mersey together with HMS *Daffodil*. The Royal Navy commandeered both vessels for action in a more dangerous role in the Zeebrugge Raid. HMS *Vindictive* was closely attended by *Iris* and *Daffodil* and entered the harbour cleverly screened by dense smoke created to the specifications of Wing Commander F.A. Brock (whose family were famous for Brock's Fireworks). Brock was present at Zeebrugge and was killed there. When the wind suddenly changed direction the ships were revealed in brilliant light from German star shells.

Daffodil's task was to keep *Vindictive* close against the mole so that storming parties could climb on. But the swell and German firepower was such that eventually there were only two specially constructed ramps in action. *Iris* was the most unfortunate vessel meeting with nothing but bad luck. Some forty minutes were spent endeavouring to secure the vessel to the mole so that raiding parties could go ashore but it was hopeless and she fell back alongside *Vindictive* hoping the men might get ashore over that vessel's deck. But by this time the block-ships were in position and the recall was sounded over the hooters. Then *Iris* took up a position astern of *Vindictive* but came under increasing fire. A large shell tore through the deck and exploded in a part of the ship where fifty-six marines were crowded together; forty-nine were killed outright and the remaining seven were wounded.

Two lives were also lost while the *Iris* was close to the mole. It was for this heroic action that Lieutenant Commander George Nicholson Bradford was awarded a posthumous Victoria Cross. In many accounts Bradford's exploits are described first while Lieutenant Claude Ernest Vincent Hawkings' actions come second. But in the official citation for Bradford's VC, it is Hawkings' heroism that comes first. The citation states that 'great difficulty was experienced in placing parapet-anchors owing to the motion of the ship', and so there was an attempt to use scaling ladders before the ship was secured. Hawkings: 'managed to get one ladder in position and actually reached the parapet, the ladder being crushed to pieces just as he stepped off it. This very gallant young officer was last seen defending himself with his revolver. He was killed on the parapet.' He was 22.

Then follows Bradford's exploit. Although securing the ship was not part of his duties, he climbed up the derrick that carried a large parapet-anchor. He awaited his chance while the ship surged up and down, then jumped onto the mole with the anchor and placed it in position. But he was riddled with machine-gun bullets and the anchor tore away.

Hawkings was the youngest son of Mr and Mrs Percy Hawkings of 49 The Drive. He was educated at Marlborough House School in The Drive and his name appears on the school's memorial plaque inside All Saints Church, Hove. He entered the Navy as a Cadet in May 1908 and he also served aboard HMS *Orion* at the Battle of Jutland. Although their actions at Zeebrugge were similar, it seems rather unfair that Hawkings was Mentioned in Despatches while his superior officer received the coveted Victoria Cross. But the authorities were in a dilemma with so many brave and heroic actions to be considered. They fell back on the Royal Warrant procedure, which stated a ballot should take place when there were several men who were all eligible for this decoration and thus not all those nominated for a Victoria Cross received one.

The 4th Battalion Royal Marines were badly affected by the Zeebrugge Raid and out of a force of 1,000 men, only seventy-five marched back to Chatham Barracks, the others either killed or wounded. But taking the whole expedition into consideration, the loss

British minesweepers moored at Zeebrugge. (Author)

of 10 per cent of personnel was considered good and even remarkable, given the circumstances. The Bruges canal was successfully blocked and it was to take three weeks of furious dredging by the Germans to partially re-open a channel. In a wartime situation those three weeks were a precious breathing space, besides the raid being a great boost to British morale. The success of the raid was only to become apparent much later as aerial reconnaissance could not pinpoint the cleverly camouflaged places affected. It would have been even more of a success had the RAF taken advantage of the situation at once by taking out the blocked-in ships. But unhappily for the Navy, the end of March 1918 was the end of the Royal Naval Air Service as it combined with the Royal Flying Corps to become the Royal Air Force. The raid on Ostend planned to take place at the same time as Zeebrugge was a failure due to a moved buoy, but a later raid in May had some success.

Notes

5. Hove Box Library 2

CHAPTER 8

Counting the Cost – The Army

Of the 642 names recorded on Hove's Roll of Honour as having died in the Great War, 163 were members of the Royal Sussex Regiment. The regiment expanded rapidly during this time, was composed of twenty-three battalions and served in all theatres of war, although the 1st Battalion remained stationed in India. The 2nd Battalion was the first to see action as they were sent to France in August 1914 with the 1st Division and there they remained for the duration of the war, suffering a loss of 1,723 officers and men. The 3rd (Militia) Battalion was based in Newhaven and served as a depot for reinforcements; the 4th Battalion was active in Gallipoli, Egypt and Palestine and the Western Front; the 5th Battalion was in France and Italy; while the 7th, 8th and 9th Battalions, plus the three Southdown Battalions, fought in France. The Sussex Yeomanry became the 16th Battalion and served in Palestine and on the Western Front. Four Victoria Crosses were won by the regiment, two of them by officers of the 2nd Battalion. In Chichester Cathedral the Regimental Chapel of St George displays panels recording the names of 6,800 members who died in the Great War.

Many of the young recruits to the Royal Sussex Regiment must have had similar experiences to George Parker. When war broke out, Parker was working at the Co-op in Blatchington Road, Hove. His family lived at 74 Hanover Terrace, Brighton, and to save money he walked all the way to work and back again. He was too young to

This card carries a patriotic sentiment 'Rally to the Flag'. But as war dragged on it came to the point when volunteers were no longer enough, and conscription had to be introduced. (Author)

This silk card carries the poignant message 'a kiss from the trenches'. It would be difficult to find anything more different from the delicate stitching of the card to contrast with the glutinous mud of the trenches. (Author)

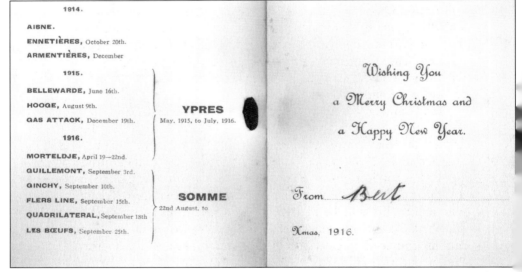

1914.		
AISNE.		
ENNETIÈRES, October 20th.		
ARMENTIÈRES, December		
1915.		
BELLEWARDE, June 16th.		
HOOGE, August 9th.	**YPRES**	
GAS ATTACK, December 19th.	May. 1915, to July, 1916.	
1916.		
MORTELDJE, April 19—22nd.		
QUILLEMONT, September 3rd.		
GINCHY, September 10th.		
FLERS LINE, September 15th.	**SOMME**	
QUADRILATERAL, September 18th	22nd August, to	
LES BŒUFS, September 25th.		

Wishing You a Merry Christmas and a Happy New Year.

From Bert

Xmas, 1916.

There cannot have been a great choice of Christmas cards when this regimental creation was sent to Mabel Sharp with the season's greetings. (D. Sharp)

volunteer for the forces but began to feel left out. One Wednesday afternoon on his half-day off, he suddenly decided to visit 20 Church Road, Hove, where he found a recruiting sergeant, an officer and a medical officer. When asked his age he replied '18' and the perceptive

On Christmas Day 1914 an extraordinary event took place when German and British soldiers fraternized in No Man's Land. On Christmas Eve the 39th Garhwalis of the Indian Army were surprised to see small Christmas trees with lighted candles appear on top of the parapet belonging to German trenches. They said it reminded them of their own festival of Diwali. (Author)

sergeant enquired if his mother knew he was that age. In fact he was 15 but no matter, he passed his medical, took the oath of allegiance and received the King's shilling. His call-up arrived several months later. He went to the regiment's headquarters at Chichester Barracks where a typically tough sergeant endeavoured to turn raw recruits into soldiers. Uniforms and equipment were issued but puttees were puzzling until a kindly regular soldier told them how to put them on. Lads like Parker, who came from a deprived background, flourished during the days of training. There were physical workouts, bayonet training, runs and marching, all in the fresh air, plus regular meals. Many of the patriotic recruits were puny and stunted in growth.

After training, Parker travelled from Folkestone to Calais and on to the Belgium town of Poperinghe, known to British troops as 'Pops', and not far from Ypres, nicknamed 'Wipers'. By this time Parker was attached to the 3/Sherwood Foresters, which suffered many losses at Ypres. The soldiers moved up the line in the dark, treading gingerly on duckboards that were only 18 inches wide. Parker slipped off into the mud and by the time he had extricated himself, his companions had vanished. Conditions were harsh, drinking water was tainted and food rations limited. Sometimes they subsisted on horsemeat and bread. Parker and two companions contracted diphtheria and returned to England in a hospital ship. It was touch and go for Parker but eventually he pulled through.

Parker returned to the front line at the Somme after completing a machine-gun course. He later joined the 46th Division in time for the big push to take Thiepval. In the midst of battle and due to high casualties, Parker was promoted to corporal and was in charge of a Lewis and machine-gun section. When they drew near to Thiepval they

Soldiers of the Machine Gun Corps ride to the Front in motor lorries. In 1914 British and Indian troops were amused at the arrival of thirty-six red London buses still adorned with the usual adverts for use as troop transports. (*Illustrated London News* 2 November 1918)

came under heavy machine-gun fire and his platoon officer, Lieutenant Shackleton, Parker and his section went forward to flush out the machine-gun nest. For their gallant actions, Lieutenant Shackleton was awarded the Military Cross while Parker won the Military Medal. The two were fortunate to survive but both had to visit the dressing station, Parker to have grenade pieces removed from his thigh and abdomen.

There was fierce fighting as they advanced, including hand-to-hand combat, and it was no easier when they went beyond the Hindenburg Line. There were so many casualties he was promoted to sergeant on the battlefield. On 17 October 1918 he sustained injuries to his knee and hip and returned to England aboard the hospital ship *Aberdonian*. But after four years of war and still only 20 years old, he was lucky to be alive. He lived to the age of 73 and it was only after his death that his daughter discovered a manuscript outlining his experiences. He had never spoken to her about the war.

Like George Parker, Ernie Mason pretended he was older than he was so that he could enlist. He was based at the Sussex County Cricket Ground where there was a Drill Hall. He was in the 6th (Cyclist) Battalion Royal Sussex Regiment, but it must have been difficult to balance on such a heavy bicycle encumbered with a rifle clipped to one side of the frame. Like Parker he too started off in the Royal Sussex Regiment but men were sent to different regiments wherever there was the most need. On one occasion he startled his family by arriving home on leave wearing a kilt, having been assigned to the London Scottish Regiment. He served in the trenches and ended his military career in southern Ireland with the Black and Tans.

Bert Healey finished his schooling at the age of 14 but was fortunate in obtaining an apprenticeship as an electrician's mate when he was 15. He worked for the well-known firm of Banfield's, engineers and stores. There was a shop in Western Road, Hove, and the works were tucked away in Brunswick Street East. He remained there for a year, then he became bored and thought it would be an exciting life in the Army. Although he was not 18 years old, he was a large lad and had no difficulty in being accepted at the recruiting office. He too was sent to Chichester Barracks. He joined the Royal Engineers and disillusion quickly set in. He could not handle a heavy vehicle and was told he needed more practical experience. He realized his future was mapped out as a 'grease boy', a prospect he did not relish. He wrote to his father saying he wanted to come home. His father went to the recruiting office in Waterloo Place and told them the facts. Soon young Healey was facing an irate sergeant major for a good ticking-off, then he was handed a railway warrant, his earnings of six shillings and off he went. His army career lasted all of two months.

During the Great War, fighting surged back and forth around Ypres in Belgium, causing dreadful damage to the town and the deaths of several local men. Sir Arthur Conan Doyle visited Ypres in 1916 and wrote it was 'destroyed, deserted and desecrated but with a sad, proud dignity, which made you lower your voice as you passed through the ruined streets'.

The first battle of Ypres lasted from 12 October to 22 November 1914, when the German army attempted to break through the allied front. Although British casualties amounted to more than 50,000 soldiers, it was a modest loss when compared with the carnage to come.

These local men died during the battle:

Private Edwin Read, 2/Royal Sussex*
6 November – Corporal Herbert George Clevett, 2/Royal Sussex, died of wounds

Ruined Ypres produced such a melancholy effect that Sir Arthur Conan Doyle felt you needed to lower your voice when passing through. (Author)

8 November – Private Walter George Etherington 2/Royal Sussex (seconded from North Staffordshire Regiment)*
13 November – Private Percy George Coomber, 7/Royal Sussex
15 November – Private Reginald Coomber, 2/Royal Sussex*
18 November – Second Lieutenant Lawrence Ernest Pelham Grubb 2/Royal Sussex (seconded from King's Own Yorkshire Light Infantry)*
30 November – Private Richard Parker, 2/Royal Sussex*
20 December – Lieutenant Jean François Constantin Maxime de Crevaisier, Baron de Vomécourt

(The asterisk denotes that their names are inscribed at the Menin Gate, Ypres, and the men have no known grave.)

Private Reginald Coomber was born at 75 Clarendon Road on 23 September 1899 and educated at Ellen Street Schools. When he grew up he still lived in the same road but at number 78 and worked as a labourer. He enlisted in 1912 and was killed by a sniper at Ypres.

Private Edwin Read was born at 22 Ellen Street on 12 January 1884 and educated at East Hove Schools. He enlisted in 1901 and held the

Sir Reginald Blomfield (1856-1942) designed the impressive Menin Gate.
(Author)

South African War medal. He later earned his living as a platelayer for the Railway Company and was a married man living at 115 Livingstone Road at the outbreak of war. His family were informed that the exact date of his death could not be ascertained but it was between 31 October and 2 November.

Lieutenant Jean Francois Constantin Maxime de Crevaisier, Baron de Vomécourt, was born in 1863 in the Vosges area of France, educated at the Collège de Nancy and the University of Paris. He joined the 6 Regiment D'Artillerie de Campagne on 20 October 1914 and died at Ypres exactly two months later. He had a house at 76 The Drive, Hove.

The second battle of Ypres took place from 22 April to 25 May 1915 and was memorable for being the first time Germans employed chlorine gas.

These local men died:

24 April – Private William Bernard Dancy, 1st Canadian Division*
26 April – Lieutenant Colonel Henry William Ernest Hitchins
26 April – Private Henry Walter Millington, Hampshire Regiment*
26 April – Private Frederick Herbert Tomlins, Middlesex Regiment*
24 May – Lieutenant John Cecil Stollery, Warwickshire Regiment*
24/25 May – Second Lieutenant Frederick Athelstan Fanshawe Baines*

25 May – Private Morgan Henry Mason, 1/ Welsh Regiment*
16 June – Private Gerald Enrico Pearse, Honourable Artillery Company*

Second Lieutenant Baines of the 4/King's Royal Rifle Corps was aged 19 when he was killed in action. His military career was heartbreakingly brief – he joined his battalion on Sunday and died on Tuesday. His parents received several letters of condolence from friends and colleagues. The following is quoted from Captain Grattan-Bellew's letter:

> I only knew your son for a week but even so had time to get very fond of him […] We travelled up together to the Front, having a very cheery time. In fact while we were waiting on the road near Ypres for orders to advance we had a game of Bridge together with Mr Ballance. We all knew that night what was before us and I don't think any of us expected to come out of it […] On Monday morning we were called out to attack some trenches the Germans had from us that morning by the use of gas. We came under fire about midnight. I was in command of the first line and your son was with the third line […] My line was badly cut up and scattered in front of the German trenches and apparently your son's line met the same fate; and it was then he was killed. Last time I saw him he was in great spirits and as cool as the oldest hand there. A few of my Company were in his line and spoke most highly of his behaviour under one of the hottest fires seen in the war. He died about the best possible death for an officer, without a thought for himself, only for his men.

His old headmaster from Winchester College wrote: 'This is the saddest blow I have felt so far; he was such a wholesome, honourable and attractive fellow, truly a white soul, if ever there was one. Everyone was admiring him when he stayed here only thirteen days ago.'

His father Athelstan Arthur Baines was a member of legal firm of Fitzhugh, Woolley, Baines and Woolley of 3 Pavilion Buildings, Brighton, and his mother Katherine Mary was the eldest daughter of Revd Frederick Fanshawe. Another relative was Lieutenant Colonel

Second Lieutenant Frederick Athelstan Fanshawe Baines was killed in action in 1915 during the Second Battle of Ypres. This is his memorial in All Saints Church, Hove.
(Author)

The war memorial inside All Saints Church, Hove, is flanked with the flags of the Royal British Legion. (Author)

Cuthbert Athelstan Baines of 41 Medina Villas, Hove. Second Lieutenant Baines' parents lived at 29 First Avenue, Hove, and later at the Old Rectory in Westmeston, Sussex. The house ceased to have a connection with the church of St Martin when the parishes of Westmeston and Streat were joined in 1909.

Inside All Saints Church, Hove, there is a handsome tablet commemorating Second Lieutenant Baines embellished with an inset coat of arms. Underneath in elaborate lettering is *Dulce et Decorum est Pro Patria Mori* (it is sweet and glorious to die for one's country). It seems likely this famous quotation from Horace owed more to a classical education rather than being an endorsement of Wilfrid Owen's bitter poem with the same title. In St Martin's Church, Westmeston there is another memorial inscription to Second Lieutenant Baines on the north wall, a stained glass window bearing his name and a further mention on the church's Roll of Honour.

Private Dancy was born at Hove in 1899 but when war broke out he was a fruit grower in Canada. On 7 August 1914 he enlisted in the 7(British Columbia) Battalion 1st Canadian Division. He was killed in action on the notorious Hill 60 near Ypres.

Lieutenant Colonel Hitchins was born in 1865 and educated privately before proceeding to Sandhurst. He became a second lieutenant in 1886 in the 1st Battalion, Manchester Regiment and was a captain by 1895. In November 1897 he was appointed adjutant of the volunteers attached to his regiment and increased membership from 600 to 1,000. During this time it was said of him: 'He was one of the most genial and loveable of men, invariably got the best out of those under him and many of his subordinates could tell of countless kindnesses performed.'[6] In 1906 he went to India with his regiment and was present for the magnificent Coronation Durbar. He enjoyed his time in India, taking a keen interest in polo and hunting. He was known as a fine horseman and a keen judge of horses. By 1914 he had been promoted to major and in the absence of the lieutenant colonel took command of the 1st Battalion, Manchester Regiment. He then had the task of mobilizing the regiment for war service and in August he left India with the 3rd (Lahore) Indian Division, arriving in France on 26 September 1914.

On 20 December 1914 Hitchins was with the 1st Manchesters when they re-took Givenchy and two lines of enemy trenches. The critical action lasting for thirty consecutive hours. It was noted that 'he was quite fearless and heedless of himself but was all the time thinking of his men'.[6] For his actions at Givenchy he was Mentioned in Despatches. He was also shot through the thigh, necessitating his return to hospital in England. On 10 March 1915 he was appointed lieutenant colonel of his own regiment and by 1 April was deemed fit enough to return to the Front. During the second Battle of Ypres he was 'brave as a lion' and was again Mentioned in Despatches. But on 26 April 'the gallant colonel of the gallant Manchesters' was shot through the heart. 'He possessed those qualities, which made men trust him in a crisis, his coolness and imperturbability in action won the admiration of all ranks.'[6]

He came from a military background, being the only son of Major General Hitchins. His mother was said to be one of the oldest residents of Hove and lived at East Lodge, Belmont. This area of Hove parish was something of an anomaly because it protruded into the environs of Brighton east of Dyke Road. In the 1920s, when the border between the two towns was rationalized Belmont was added to Brighton. There is a bronze plaque to the memory of Lieutenant Colonel Hitchins inside the church at Lynsted Village, Kent, placed there 'in memory of a much loved cousin' by a lady with a spectacular surname, Mary Vivian Roper-Lumley-Holland. There is a sad story behind the plaque because Lieutenant Colonel Hitchins was due to marry the lady.

Lieutenant Colonel Henry William Ernest Hitchins was killed in action at the Second Battle of Ypres on 26 April 1915. (Hove Library)

Private Mason was 16 years old when he died. He attended Portslade Industrial School and his father was Corporal G.H. Mason of the Scots Guards.

Lieutenant Stollery was the only son of Colonel and Mrs Stollery of 47 Denmark Villas. He was considered to be a delicate child and was not sent off to endure the rigours of boarding school. Instead he went daily first to Holland House and then to Cottesmore, both in Hove. When he eventually arrived at Christ Church, Oxford, it was recognized he was at a disadvantage because he did not have the public school old boy network to support him, but he soon settled in and made friends with many of the Rhodes scholars. In 1911 he was called to the Bar and joined the Royal Fusiliers in 1914. After fighting at Armentiers the same year, he was invalided home but returned to the Front in May 1915, attached to the Warwickshire Regiment. He came through some fierce fighting at Ypres unscathed when a large number of men in his platoon were killed or wounded. His unit was sent back for ten days rest before returning to battle. On 24 May 1915 they were ordered to re-take trenches the Germans had overcome by the use of gas. The men gallantly took the first trench and Stollery was giving orders to his men when a sniper shot him through the head at a place the British nicknamed Mousetrap Farm, near Ypres.

Although Corporal George Harry Hopkins of the 1st Life Guards was killed in action at Klein Zillebeke on 6 November 1916, and therefore does not fall within the Battle of Ypres categories, Zillebeke is less than 2 miles south east of Ypres and he deserves a mention. There was a fierce battle at this location and German gunners hidden in woods hampered British actions. Afterwards there were only six officers left in the 1st Life Guards and four in the 2nd Life Guards. Corporal Hopkins was shot in the head. That night Squadron Corporal Major Robert W. Sensier wrote a letter to Hopkins' sister:

Lieutenant John Cecil Stollery was killed in action at the Second Bat of Ypres on 24 May 191. (Hove Library)

> When we lost your brother, Miss Hopkins, we lost someone who it seemed we could never replace. We always spoke of him as our Happy Corporal. He always seemed to be laughing and he was brave as he was happy. Nothing was too much trouble for him; he was a typical big-hearted British soldier. He had spoken to me of his wife (if I remember right she is an invalid). I'm so sorry for her but trust she will be cared for.

Hopkins had been a professional soldier since 1903 and was a time-expired man, so when he enlisted in August 1914 it was as a reservist. Between his two stints in the Army, he was employed by the Brighton & Hove Bus Company and lived at Hove.

Another Hove man killed in action at Zillebeke on 2 August 1916 was Lieutenant Kenneth Fleetwood Gordon Pinhey of the Royal Artillery. He came from an interesting family. His father was Lieutenant Colonel Sir Alexander Fleetwood Pinhey, Indian Army, who served in the sub-continent and in 1910 was private secretary to the

Viceroy, 4th Earl of Minto. Lieutenant
Pinhey's mother, Lady Violet Beatrice, was
the daughter of Sir Henry William Gordon,
brother to the famous General Charles
George Gordon (1833-1885) who died
heroically at Khartoum. Lieutenant Pinhey
was born in India on 23 July 1896 and as his
parents continued to live in Hyderabad, he
stayed with his aunt Miss Gordon at 27
Wilbury Road, Hove, when he came to
England. It was at this address that Lady
Violet died in 1916. The Gordon connection
with the Hove house continued until the late
1930s and in 1933 Hove Museum celebrated
the centenary of General Gordon's birth by
mounting a special exhibition with relics lent
by Miss Gordon and Colonel L.A. Gordon,
including the tools General Gordon took to
China.

*Lieutenant Kenneth Fleetwood
Gordon Pinhey was killed in
action at Zillebeke on 2 August
1916.* (Hove Library)

*Lieutenant Pinhey's
great-uncle was the
famous General
Gordon of Khartoum.
The Gordon family
home was at 27
Wilbury Road, Hove.*
(Author)

Seated on the wreckage of a German gun a non-commissioned officer calmly eats his dinner. (*Illustrated London News* 21 October 1916)

This wonderfully clear depiction of an officer at the Front was accompanied by an advertisement. Such a picture gave the folks back home an idealized view of the conflict. (*Illustrated London News* 21 October 1916)

The third battle of Ypres was fought from 31 July to 10 November 1917 and was also known as the Battle of Passchendaele. It was carried out in dreadful conditions because the ground was a sea of mud due to successive artillery bombardments. The loss of life was horrific especially since British troops only managed an advance of 5 miles at a cost of 250,000 casualties. The objective was to break through German lines in order to reach and destroy German submarine bases on the Belgian coast, and the failure to do so was one reason for the Zeebrugge Raid of 1918.

The following local men perished in the battle:

31 July – Private Jefferys Somerset Allen, Middlesex Regiment, attached to the Cambridgeshire Regiment*

31 July – Lieutenant Howis Hillman, Rifle Brigade*

31 July – Private George Alfred Maslen, 13/Royal Sussex

31 July – Guardsman Stanley Fullalove Newell, 2/Grenadier Guards.

31 July – Private Frederick E. Streeter, Welsh Regiment*

31 July – Private Alfred Thomas West, 8/Royal Sussex.

1 August – Private Alfred Percy Blann, 13/ Royal Sussex, aged 27*

3 August – Sergeant Francis William Jestico, 9/Royal Sussex

4 August – Private John Henry Gorton, Middlesex Regiment*

6 August – Sapper Reginald Albert Cole, Royal Engineers*

10 August – Private Joseph Bernard Walsh, Royal Fusiliers*

16 August – Captain Edgar Hazel Hester, Royal Inniskillin Fusiliers

16 August – Second Lieutenant Charles Hawkins Inwood, Machine Gun Corps

16 August – Captain Reginald Cuthbert Welsford Smithers, KOYLI

5 September – Private Albert Frank Strevens, 8/Royal Sussex, Polygon Wood*

6 September – Major Henry Griffith Boone, DSO, Royal Field Artillery

8 September – Sergeant Horace Reginald Diplock, MM, DCM, 8/Royal Sussex

9 September – Lance Corporal Eric Simon, Royal West Kent
Regiment

20 September – Private William Strickels Hopkins, 1/London Regiment

20 September – Private Ernest Victor Townsend, 12/Royal
Sussex**

20 September – Second Lieutenant Kenneth Martin Wearne,
Royal West Surrey Regiment**

25 September – Lance Corporal George Knee, 12/Royal Sussex**

26 September – Private Herbert Jupp, 11/Royal Sussex

26 September – Sergeant Herbert John Maslin, Sussex Yeomanry,
attached to the Middlesex Regiment**

26 September – Lance-Corporal George Henry Oram, 13/Royal
Sussex

27 September – Trooper Sydney Thomas George Welling,
11/Royal Sussex, Polygon Wood**

14 October – Lance Corporal John Boxall, Royal Sussex
(Pioneers)

19 October – Private Bernard John Blaber, 11/Royal Sussex

30 October – Gunner Harold Edward Matthews, Royal Garrison
Artillery

30 October – Private Herbert Wakeley White, Canadian Light
Infantry*

6 November – Corporal Cecil Charles King, died of wounds
received at Ypres

6 November – Private Arthur Aaron Short died of wounds
received at Ypres

16 November – Bombardier Herbert Mallett Caddy, Royal Field
Artillery

(The single asterisk denotes the name is inscribed on the Menin
Gate while a double asterisk denotes the name is inscribed at the
Tyne Cot Memorial to the Missing and the men have no known
grave.)

Bombardier William Barker joined the 54 Battery/Royal Field Artillery
on 24 November 1908 and was stationed at Preston Barracks for a
while before coming to Hove in 1914 where he and his wife lived at
33 Blatchington Road. He served in France from 17 August 1914,

seeing action at Mons and Ypres, and was wounded. He took part in the Gallipoli campaign in 1915 but had to be invalided home suffering from enteric fever and dysentery. When he recovered he went back to France where he served from January 1916 to August 1917 but at Ypres he contracted pleurisy and was sent home. He was at Trent Bridge Military Hospital, Nottingham, for six months before he died on 25 February 1918.

Private Alfred Percy Blann was killed in action at the Third Battle of Ypres on 1 August 1917. (Hove Library)

Private Blaber worked as a carter for a local farm in civilian life and lived at 102 Wordsworth Street. He enlisted in February 1916.

Private Blann was born at Worthing but by 1914 he lived at 23 Lansdowne Street and earned a living as a grocer. He enlisted on 30 December 1914 but was killed in action at St Julien.

Major Boone was born in India in 1880 and was the son of Colonel F.B. Boone, Madras Staff Corps, and Mrs Boone of 7 Langdale Road. He was educated at Wellington and then at the Royal Military Academy, Woolwich. He obtained his commission on 6 January 1900 and was sent first to Gibraltar and then to India to join a mountain battalion. While he was in India he became a first class polo player and won many trophies. In 1904 he was part of the Tibet Expedition and received the Tibet Medal and clasp. On return to England he exchanged into the Royal Field Artillery and in 1914 was acting adjutant. He was sent to France in August 1914 and saw plenty of action, including the Battle and Retreat from Mons. On 15 September he was wounded in the Battle of Aisne and invalided home to recuperate. He returned to the Front a year later. He was twice Mentioned in Despatches and was awarded the DSO for 'distinguished service and personal bravery under fire'. He was mortally wounded at Ypres on 5 September 1917, 'when regardless of everything but his duty, he went to look after the safety and welfare of his men during heavy shelling'.[7] He died the next day at Proven in Belgium.

Lance Corporal Boxall was born at Hove in 1892, educated at Portland Road Schools and lived at 10 Malvern Street. He worked as a shop assistant before enlisting in the Royal Sussex in September 1914. He became the company writer and was killed by a bomb dropped from an enemy aircraft. The captain wrote to his mother: 'He was unique; no detail was too small for his thorough way; no duty too irksome; and no task too dangerous. You have lost a dear and noble son, beloved of all his comrades, one of the original battalion stock.'

A bursting shell killed Bombardier Hubert Mallett Caddy of the Royal Field Artillery. He joined the Army on 20 May 1916 as a gunner and was a married man with a baby boy he had only seen once. He was the son of William and Catherine Caddy of 41 Waterloo Street. Mr Caddy was a respected furniture maker and wood carver and his son also helped in the family business. W.H. Caddy taught at Hove Technical Institute and was commissioned to carve a reading desk out of solid oak for the new grammar school. He also created the trestle tables and chairs for Hove College and carved their war memorial too.

Lance Corporal Horace Hemsley was born at Wandsworth in 1891 and educated at Portslade. He was a boiler attendant and lived at 52 Ellen Street when he enlisted on 22 September 1911. He joined the Cyclist Battalion of the Royal Sussex and later transferred to the Army Cyclist Corps. He was sent to France in November 1914. On 2 August 1917 at Ypres he was awarded the Military Medal for his actions under heavy shellfire, when he extricated seven Royal Field Artillery drivers and seven Royal Engineers, dressed their wounds and despatched them to the dressing station. While he was thus engaged he was wounded in the back. But he survived and was demobbed on 18 May 1919.

Corporal Richard Charles Holmes was born at Harwich in 1882 but later moved to Hove and lived at 63 Ellen Street. He earned a living as a cabman before he enlisted in March 1915 in the 7/Royal Sussex. He was awarded the Belgian Croix de Guerre for bravery and devotion to duty on the Ypres Front in October 1917. He was also wounded and gassed, but he survived the war.

Private Hopkins, who enlisted in July 1915, did not only serve with the London Regiment; he was seconded to the 26/Royal Fusiliers and on 1 July 1916 was wounded while with the West Kents. In civilian life he was a porter and lived at 35 Bolsover Road. At Ypres a sniper shot him in the stomach.

Second Lieutenant Inwood was the second son of Revd Charles and Mrs Inwood of Hove Park Villas. At the outbreak of war he was in the USA but returned immediately and enlisted with the Royal Fusiliers (Public School Battalion). He was gazetted to the Royal Sussex and thence to the Machine Gun Corps. He took a strenuous part in the fighting at Arras and the Ypres Salient. He was informed that his servant Private Hartle had been wounded and at once he climbed out of his shell hole and went to the one where his servant lay, but he was hit in the head by a fragment of shell and died.

Sergeant Jestico was born in Brighton in 1888 and was a professional soldier, having enlisted in 1908. His parents Isaac and Annie Jestico lived at 132 Ellen Street. His brother died in the Gallipoli campaign.

Private Jupp was born in 1886. At the outbreak of war he was a married man living at 28 Ruskin Road and earned a living as a barman. He enlisted on 9 June 1915 and was killed in action at Polygon Wood.

Corporal King lived at 66 Payne Avenue with his wife. He was a gas fitter. He joined the Royal Engineers in August 1914 and he was awarded the Military Medal for gallantry in action on 3 October 1917. On 4 November 1917 he was seriously wounded in the chest at Ypres and taken to Number 3 Canadian Casualty Clearing Station where he died on 6 November 1917. The chaplain wrote to his widow: 'He asked me to send you his love. I do not think he realized how seriously ill he was.'

Private Maslen was born at Hove in 1894, but at the outbreak of war he was earning a living as a chauffeur and lived at Bolney. He joined the 13/Royal Sussex in March 1916.

Sergeant Maslin was born at Wiston in 1887, but the family later moved to Hove where young Maslin was educated at Ellen Street Schools. Before enlisting he was a blind maker and lived at 22 Clarendon Road. He joined the Sussex Yeomanry in October 1915 and was later transferred to the Middlesex Regiment.

In civilian life Gunner Matthews was a milk carrier for Frowd and Walker's Dairies at 38 Western Road, Hove. He was a married man and lived at 116 Cowper Street. He enlisted in the Royal Garrison Artillery in May 1917 and died the same year at Ypres. 'Dug out was blown in. He died in Poperinghe Hospital.'[8]

Private Frederick Joseph Messenger was born at 1 Shirley Street in

1880 and when he married, he and Edith moved down the road to 32 Shirley Street. He was educated at Connaught Road Schools. His parents lived at 11 Haddington Street where a family member continued to live until recent times. Messenger was already a sergeant in the British Red Cross when he enlisted in the Royal Army Medical Corps. He was awarded the Military Medal for rescuing the wounded under heavy shellfire on 21/22 July 1917 at Ypres. He also held a proficiency badge for service at the Indian Hospital at York Place and the Kitchener Hospital. He survived the war.

Guardsman Newell was a dental student living at Hove when he joined the 2/Grenadier Guards in November 1916. He was aged 19 when he was killed in action.

Leading Seaman Albert Jesse Saunders was born at Hove in 1892, was educated at Ellen Street Schools and later worked on a bread-round for Gigins. He enlisted in December 1915 and was in *Hood* Battalion of the Royal Naval Reserve. On 26 October 1917 he won the Military Cross for carrying in the wounded while under heavy fire at Passchendaele and he was awarded the Distinguished Conduct Medal for bombing German trenches at Cambrai on 30 December 1917. He survived the war.

Private Short was born at Hove in 1879. He joined the Army c.1898 and served for five years. He returned to England and worked as a paper-hanger for William Willett, the well-known Hove builder. Then he visited Australia where he joined the Australian Pioneers in 1915. He was twice wounded. His brother, Signaller Frederick Charles Short of the Royal West Kent Regiment, was later killed in action in France on 7 April 1918.

Lance Corporal Simon was born in Jersey in 1890. He was killed in action at Gilwell Wood, Ypres.

Reginald Cuthbert Welsford Smithers of the 7/King's Own Yorkshire Light Infantry was aged 19 but already a captain and adjutant when he was killed in action. His father was Herbert Welsford Smithers who, with his brother Edward Allfree Smithers, founded their brewery in 1906 at Brighton with the amalgamation of the North Street Brewery and Bedford Brewery. In 1913 they acquired the old firm of Vallance and Catt of the West Street Brewery to add to their portfolio. The brothers were unusually close and when Herbert died on 9 June 1913, Edward could not get over his loss and died on 5 February 1914. Their

Captain Smithers was aged 19 when he was killed in action near Ypres on 16 August 1917. This memorial tablet is in All Saints Church, Hove.
(Author)

Captain Reginald Cuthbert Welsford Smithers, King's Own Yorkshire Light Infantry. (Hove Library)

unhappy father was left with just a daughter and in memory of his sons he gave two stained glass windows in the north aisle of All Saints, Hove. Reginald and his brother Montague attended their father's funeral and burial in Hove Cemetery in 1913 and four years later Reginald was dead. His widowed mother remarried, becoming Mrs A.J. Hollick, and lived at 9 Eaton Gardens.

Lieutenant Edward Henry Keith Smithers was a cousin of Captain Smithers, being the son of Edward Allfree Smithers. The lieutenant was born on 6 January 1896 in a large house called The Gables at Furze Hill, Hove, and he was still living there eighteen years later. He was educated at nearby Wick School and later at Winchester College. He had already entered New College, Oxford, when he enlisted in

September 1914 as a second lieutenant in the 11/Manchesters, and died on 11 July 1916.

Corporal Jack Stanley Waters was educated at George Street Schools and earned a living as a butcher. He lived at 90 Rutland Road. He enlisted in the 12/Royal Sussex Regiment in September 1914 and survived the war. He was awarded the Military Medal: 'For most conspicuous gallantry and good leading in the Battle of Ypres on July 31, and August 1 and 2. While crossing No Man's Land, the NCO in charge of the Lewis Gun Team was wounded. This man at once took charge of the team and led them to their objective. During the whole period of the operation his gun was always in action, and his cheerfulness at a very critical period was of the utmost value in keeping up the spirit of the men in his section.'

Second Lieutenant Wearne was educated at Uppingham and lived at 13 Fourth Avenue while his parents lived at 22 The Drive. A handwritten note on his war record states: 'He was never found, presumably blown to pieces.'

Hove-born Private White was living in Ontario, Canada, when war broke out and he enlisted in November 1915. He was a cabinet-maker by trade.

Second Lieutenant Wearne was killed at the Third Battle of Ypres on 20 September 1917 aged 20. (Hove Library)

Seven battalions of the Royal Sussex Regiment were involved in the Battle of the Somme, which started on 1 July 1916 and turned out to be the blackest day in the annals of the British Army with the most casualties ever suffered in a single day of conflict. The number of men killed came to 19,240. The Battle of the Somme lasted until 18 November 1916. Conditions at the Somme were extremely difficult. Besides the incessant noise of artillery barrages, the strongly defended German entrenchments, the withering crossfire and the dreadfully high casualty rate, soldiers also had to put up with the annoyance of large rats scuttling about and lice infesting hair and clothes. There was a rumour that Harrison's Pomade was just the thing to get rid of lice but

Canadian soldiers in action, going over the top at the Somme. (Illustrated London News 21 October 1916)

Canadian soldiers found this little dog in Courcellete, adopted him and gave him the name Fritz. (Illustrated London News 21 October 1916)

The reverse side of this postcard of African troops on their way to the Somme in 1916 carried a programme of forthcoming attractions at the Picturedrome Cinema, North Street, Portslade. The card was sold in aid of the Blinded Soldiers' Children Fund and if yours was the lucky number you could win £1. (Author)

A scene on the Western Front with troops on the march being watched by troops at rest. (*Illustrated London News* 21 October 1916)

on the contrary they did not mind it at all. The battlefield stench of polluted mud and rotting corpses was so pervasive that it took two or three days away from the trenches before the nostrils lost the smell. The Somme was also a curious mix of the old and the new, being the last time cavalry was used in France on a large scale while the actions of the Royal Flying Corps proved to be invaluable. But if the allies suffered bad losses, so too did the Germans. The British casualties came to 420,000 while the Germans are said to have lost 650,000 men.

The following local men died at the Somme:

1 July – Private Charles Robert Adland, 2/Royal Fusiliers
1 July – Rifleman Douglas Bradford Bennett, 1/16 London Regiment*
1 July – Private Albert William Burtenshaw, 16/Middlesex Regiment*
1 July – Lance Corporal Samuel Ashburner Foot, 16/ Middlesex Regiment
1 July – Private Charles James Littlewood, 18/ King's Liverpool Regiment
1 July – Private Ernest Edward Reeves, 1/5 London Regiment*

1 July – Private Henry John Tipper, 8/East Surrey

3 July – Private Arthur Hall, 6/ Royal West Kent, Ovillers

7 July – Private Albert John Back, 7/ Royal Sussex, Ovillers*

7 July – Private Percy Mackenzie Bell, 7/Royal Sussex, Ovillers

7 July – Private Alfred William Percy Burden, 7/Royal Sussex, Ovillers

7 July – Private Gordon William Elms, 7/Royal Sussex, Ovillers

7 July – Sergeant Arthur James Evans MM, 7/Royal Sussex, Ovillers

7 July – Private Frederick William Fitch, 7/Royal Sussex, Ovillers

7 July – Private Robert Hazeldine, 7/Royal Sussex, Ovillers

7 July – Private Frederick William Jackson, 7/Royal Sussex, Ovillers

13 July – Private Charles Rothwell, 8/Royal Sussex, Bernafey Wood*

14 July – Private George John Williams Andrews, 8/Royal Sussex

19 July – Private Joseph John Lewis, 13/Cheshire Regiment*

20 July – Corporal Frank Wilkinson, 20/Royal Fusiliers, High Wood*

23 July – Private Charles Archer, 2/Royal Sussex*

23 July – Private Arthur Edwin James Prince, 17/Lancashire Fusiliers*

1 August – Corporal Walter Linden, 7/Royal Sussex*

3 August – Private Albert Ernest Stone, Royal Fusiliers

3 August – Lance Corporal Arthur Whale, 8/Royal Fusiliers, Ovillers

4 August – Private Arthur Edward Wales, 9/Royal Fusiliers*

5 August – Private Thomas George Cleveland, Royal Fusiliers

5 August – Private George Alfred John Kent, 7/Royal Sussex*

7 August – Lieutenant James Bruce North Carvic, Australian Imperial Force

8 August – Second Lieutenant George Harry Thornton Ross, Essex Regiment

13 August – Private Frederick Owen Livermore, Queen's Royal West Surrey Regiment

16 August – Private Harry Richards, 2/Royal Sussex*

18 August – Second Lieutenant Kenneth Coldwell Bright, Royal Sussex, Guillemont*

18 August – Sergeant Thomas Lee, 7/Rifle Brigade*

18 August – Private William John Minall, Machine Guns Corps

18 August – Private Arthur Charles Pettitt, 9/Royal Sussex, Guillemont*

18 August – Lance Corporal Frederick Alexander Radford, 9/Royal Sussex, Guillemont*

23 August – Private Charles Edwin Edwards MM, Australian Imperial Force

24 August – Private Alfred Alma Dunk, 1/14 Oxford & Bucks. Light Infantry*

26 August – Private Bertram Austin, 2/Royal Sussex

31 August – Second Lieutenant John Arthur Flowers, 9/Royal Sussex

31 August – Captain John Peake Knight, Royal Horse Artillery

1 September – Second Lieutenant Herbert Flowers, 8/Royal West Kent Regiment, Delville Wood

3 September – Sergeant Walter Mark Patching, 11/Royal Sussex*

3 September – Lance Corporal William Avis, 11/Royal Sussex

3 September – Lance Corporal Percy Dummer, 11/Sussex, Becourt

3 September – Private Richard George, 11/ Royal Sussex

3 September – Corporal Arthur Cyril Lee, Rifle Brigade, Becourt*

3 September – Sergeant Walter Patching, 13/Royal Sussex, Becourt Ridge

3 September – Private Arthur George Pittock, 1/Royal West Surrey*

3 September – Sergeant Reginald Ernest Smither, 11/Royal Sussex*

3 September – Company Sergeant Major Edward Stevens, 11/Royal Sussex, Becourt

4 September – Corporal Victor James Goddard MM, 6/Duke of Cornwall's Light Infantry*

5 September – Private George Thomas Stoner, Royal West Surrey, died from wounds

9 September – Rifleman Thomas Francis Fleet, London Regiment

15 September – First Class Signaller George Avis, Oxford & Bucks Light Infantry, Beaumont-Hamel

15 September – Guardsman Stanley Edgar Gubbins, Coldstream Guards, Flers

15 September – Rifleman John Frederick Holden, 8/Rifle Brigade*

17 September – Private Hugh Glyn Rees, 1/15 London Regiment*

23 September – Private Edward Frederick Barker, 13/Royal Sussex

25 September – Sergeant William David Turner, Grenadier Guards

25 September – Private Charles Maurice Woolgar, 1/East Kent, aged 19*

28 September – Private John Strange, 2/Royal Sussex, Becourt Wood

30 September – Lance Corporal Leonard Gann Knight, 7/Royal West Surrey*

30 September – Private Albert Frank Strevens, 8/East Surrey*

3 October – Sergeant Frederick John Russell, 7/Royal Sussex*

6 October – Private Robert Sydney Mace, 7/Royal Sussex*

7 October – Private Eustace Charles Crowther, 1/14 London Regiment*

7 October – Private Robert Lade Scarrett, 6/Royal West Kent*

12 October – Captain William Thomas Carter, 7/Seaforth Highlanders*

18 October – Second Lieutenant Alan Victor Cain, Hampshire Regiment

21 October – Rifleman George William Baker, Rifle Brigade

22 October – Private George Henry Laws, 13/Royal Sussex

23 October – Lieutenant Francis Arthur Joseph Oddie, 2/Royal Berkshire*

1 November – Private Reginald Banks, Royal Army Medical Corps

12 November – First Class Petty Officer Frederick Charles Townsend, *Howe* Battalion, Royal Naval Division, Beaumont-Hamel

13 November – Private William Cheslyn Callow, 24/Royal Fusiliers

13 November – Leading Seaman Samuel Wyatt, *Nelson* Battalion, 63/Royal Naval Division, Beaumont-Hamel

14 November – Private Albert Cook, 2/Royal Sussex

14 November – Sergeant James Hamilton Gordon Murray, Royal
Marines, 63/Royal Naval Division, Beaumont-Hamel

15 November – Private Guy Venour Brewer, Royal Fusiliers,
63/Royal Naval Division, Ancre

15 November – Private Arthur William Hopkins, HAC Infantry

18 November – Lance Corporal Egbert Harold Suter, 8/East
Surrey Regiment, Ancre

20 November – Corporal George William Preston, 11/Royal
Sussex, Commemorated on the Cambrai Memorial

(The asterisk denotes that the man's name is recorded on the
Thiepval Memorial to the Missing of the Somme, which means
he has no known grave. The memorial records the names of
72,191 British and South African men who died at the Somme.
The list in this book is probably not complete because sometimes
the family of the fallen did not know exactly where they died
and so 'France' or 'somewhere in France' was often written on
the service card. But it does give some idea of the devastation
caused by the Somme to many local families.)

Private William Percy Andrews was head porter at Gwydyr Mansions,
Hove, and lived in a flat numbered 10a. He joined the 4/Middlesex
Regiment on 3 June 1916 and on 13 November 1916 was seriously
wounded at Beaumont-Hamel and died at Rouen on 28 December
1916.

Lance Corporal William Avis lived at 37 Mortimer Road. Before
joining up, he worked as a billiard marker at the busy Cliftonville Hotel
next to Hove Railway Station. He died on the Somme, as did his
brother Signaller George Avis. Another brother Stoker Harry Avis had
already died aboard HMS *Good Hope* in 1914. Only one son survived.
He was Lance-Corporal Charles Avis of the Royal Engineers.

Hove-born Private Back was educated at Ellen Street Schools and
lived at 135 Clarendon Road. He earned a living as a van man before
enlisting in the 2/Royal Sussex in September 1914. His mother
received a letter dated 23 July 1916 from G. Rolfe of A Company,
7/Royal Sussex:

In answer to your letter I am sorry to have to tell you that your son is wounded and missing. He was hit while attacking a German trench on the 7 July. Since then he has not been seen or heard of so I am afraid you must be prepared for the worst. I have made enquiries of those left in his platoon but can get no definite news except that he was seen to be wounded. His captain was killed at the same time.

There was also a letter from J. Glover of C Company 6/The Buffs, dated 3 August 1916:

My friend Drummer Skinner and I found him this morning and we buried him in a respectable manner under the circumstances. I herewith enclose the remains of his things, the others of which my friend sent on to his young lady.

But it seems his body was not discovered after the war because his name appears on the Thiepval Memorial to the Missing.

Private Banks lived at 29 Waterloo Street, Hove with his wife and two young children and was an assistant master at the Park Street Schools, Brighton. He enlisted in October 1915 and died of wounds near Carnoy.

Private Barber was born at Hove in 1889 and educated at Ellen Street Schools. He became a barman and lived with his wife at 4 Mortimer Road. Originally he was in the 11/Royal Sussex but was seconded to another battalion.

Private Barker lived at 172 Sackville Road and was a cashier before enlisting on 24 March 1916. He was killed at Beaumont-Hamel.

Private Bell was born in 1888. He lived at Hove and was a widower. His mother lived at 2 Wilbury Crescent and his sister, Miss Bell, was matron of the Lady Chichester Hospital at 70 Brunswick Place. (This was before it moved to New Church Road.) Bell enlisted in August 1914 and joined the 7/Royal Sussex.

Rifleman Bennett was born at Brighton in 1888. He earned a living as a grocer and lived at 27 Davigdor Road. On 17 June 1915 he enlisted in the 16/London Queen's Westminster Rifles and was posted missing on 1 July. It was presumed he was killed at Gommecourt.

Private Brewer died from wounds received at Beaumont-Hamel. He was born in London in 1890 and later lived at 17 Pembroke Avenue. After he had passed his final examination enabling him to become a chartered accountant, he attempted to join the Artists' Rifles and Inns of Court Officer Training Corps, but was rejected on medical grounds. He then joined the 7/Royal Fusiliers in January 1916 and within months was dead.

Private Burden was born at Hove in 1895 and educated at George Street Schools. He worked as a shop assistant at some general stores before he enlisted in August 1914.

Second Lieutenant Alan Victor Cain was killed at the Somme on 18 October 1916. (Hove Library)

Second Lieutenant Cain was born on 12 January 1892. He joined the Hampshire Carabiniers at the outbreak of war, serving with them until February 1915 when he received a commission. He was attached to the Hampshire Regiment and served with the 29th Division in the Gallipoli Campaign, where for a time he also acted as an observer in the Royal Naval Air Service. While serving in the trenches he was severely incapacitated with frostbite and rheumatism and was invalided first to Malta and afterwards home to recuperate. When he had recovered he was despatched to the Western Front in France and from July 1916 served with the 2/Hampshires. The day before he went into battle he attended a celebration of Holy Communion in the trenches. He had a premonition of his death on the Somme and wrote to his family: 'I am only [doing] what thousands of other fellows are doing and my only anxiety is that I may not fail at the critical moment as so many other lives depend on my steadiness.' He was killed in action but it was a swift death as he was shot through the heart.

Private William Callow was born in 1893 and his brother Private Edward Callow was born in 1895, both at Hove. They earned a living as printers at 20 Church Road (corner of

Private William Cheslyn Callow was killed at the Somme on 13 November 1916 (Hove Library)

Second Avenue). Their parents lived at 41 Cambridge Road. Edward joined the 9/Royal Sussex and was killed in action at Loos in February 1915. William enlisted in March 1916 and was killed in action at the Somme.

Captain Carter was born in Kent in 1892 and educated at Hove High School and Shoreham Grammar School. He was employed as a clerk at the Anglo South American Bank in London before joining the Seaforth Highlanders in August 1914. He was killed in action leading his company at Eaucourt L'Abbaye, Somme. His parents lived in Silverdale Road and his mother, Rose Carter, wrote: 'My son was recommended by his colonel and the brigadier general for a permanent commission in the regular army and this was granted on 2 December 1916 (two months after his death). His colonel reported that he was a first class company leader and very much liked.'

Private Cook was born at Kemp Town in 1897 and educated at St Andrew's School, Portslade. By 1914 he lived at 10 St Leonard's Road and worked as a decorator.

Private Crowther lived at 8 Modena Road. He ran his own business as a wholesale stationer, printer and paper bag manufacturer. He enlisted on 1 May 1916 and was killed in action five months later, leaving a widow and two girls aged 29 months and 16 months.

Second Lieutenant Herbert Flowers was born in Steyning on 25 November 1879. He obtained a BA from Hertford College, Oxford and became a solicitor, going into partnership with his father at Steyning although he lived with his sister at 8 Salisbury Road, Hove. He was a man of many hobbies including ornithology and photography. In September 1914 he joined the 8/West Kent Regiment but was killed in action on the Somme.

Private George was born on 19 February 1894 at 123 Livingstone Road and attended Ellen Street Schools. He was a mechanic by trade and an enthusiastic club footballer, being captain of the Glendale Football Club, champions of the Hove and District League. His parents had no less than six sons serving in the Army, but it seems he was the only one to be killed in action. Perhaps

Second Lieutenant Herbert Flowers was killed at the Somme on 1 September 1916. (Hove Library)

as a precaution they had all joined different regiments: Royal Fusiliers; Royal Engineers; Ordnance Corps; Royal Army Medical Corps; and the Rifle Brigade.

Private Hopkins lived at 71 Carlisle Road and was a draper's assistant. He enlisted in November 1915 but was killed at Beaumont-Hamel.

Private Jackson was born in 1893. By 1914 he lived at 31 Prinsep Road and was a confectioner before enlisting in September 1914.

Sergeant Burnam Kelly was born in London in 1890 and became a professional soldier, enlisting in the South Wales Borderers in 1906. He was present at the siege of Tsingtao (a German port in China) in 1914, fighting with the Japanese as allies against the Germans. He served all through the Gallipoli campaign and afterwards in Egypt at El Hubri near Port Said. On the first day of the Battle of the Somme a gunshot fractured his left leg. He was awarded the Military Medal for gallant conduct leading an attack, behaving with coolness under very trying circumstances and saving a position, which was very insecure, for a considerable time. He survived the war.

Captain Knight was born at Brighton in 1890 and opted for a military career, joining the Royal Horse Artillery, T Battery, attached to the 7th Division. He received his commission in December 1910. He was twice Mentioned in Despatches, the first time in October 1914 by Lord French. When he was awarded the Distinguished Service Order on 10 November 1914, 'for great courage and initiative on several occasions', he received the medal from King George V on the battlefield. By August 1916 he was acting major in command of 35 Battery/Royal Field Artillery. He married Olivia, daughter of John Gray Knight, and they had a daughter. He was the grandson of John Peake Knight, general manager of the London, Brighton and South Coast Railway for many years.

Lance Corporal Knight was a solicitor's clerk who lived at Hove. He was a good cricket player and 'had a very wide experience of the musical world and was for some considerable time the Brighton correspondent of *The Musical Standard,* which position he filled with ability and knowledge until relinquishing his duties to join the colours'.[8] He enlisted in March 1916 in the Royal Sussex but was later attached to the Royal West Surrey Regiment. Apparently the official date of death was given as 28 September 1916 but this was disputed by a friend who was in the same battle and said Knight died on 30 September, and this friend was not far away from him at the time and was the first to communicate the news.

Corporal Lee was a hosier by trade before he enlisted in May 1915 and joined the 16/Rifle Brigade. His parents lived at 27 Prinsep Road. He was killed at Beaumont-Hamel.

Private Littlewood was born in 1889 and at the outbreak of war lived at 43 Sackville Road. By a strange coincidence he was also a hosier, just like Corporal Lee. Littlewood enlisted in August 1914.

Private Livermore was born at Hove and educated at Ellen Street Schools. When he grew up he went into service, being a footman, and lived at 62 Conway Street. He lost no time in volunteering to join the Army in September 1914.

Private Mace worked as a furniture salesman at Palmeira House. He originally enlisted in the Sussex Yeomanry but was transferred to the Royal Sussex. He was only 19 when he was killed.

Sergeant James Hamilton Gordon Murray was in the Royal Marines Divisional Engineers. He was born in Castle Douglas on 28 December 1885 and attended Alloa Academy. He was the great-grandson of Major John Murray of Peninsular fame who married the Honourable Miss Hamilton, daughter of the fourth son of the Duke of Abercorn. Sergeant Murray's mother later moved to Hove where she lived at 34 Brunswick Square. At the outbreak of war Murray was in Canada and earning a living as an electrical engineer but felt compelled to return to the old country and volunteer. He joined up in August 1914 as a sapper. His superiors thought he deserved a commission and he received several offers but always turned them down. But he was not without valour and received the Distinguished Service Medal as well as being Mentioned in Despatches by General Sir Ian Hamilton. At Gallipoli on 4 June 1915, 'Sapper Murray was called upon to repair a defective field cable line between Divisional Headquarters and the support lines and found the cable broken in no less than ten places but by dint of perseverance he repaired the cable and finally re-established communication. The whole of the work was carried out under considerable rifle fire in exposed positions [...] the repairs occupied three hours.' Murray became part of the 63rd Royal Naval Division and was killed in action on 14 November 1916 at Beaumont-Hamel.

Sergeant James Hamilton Gordon Murray was killed at the Somme on 14 November 1916. (Hove Library)

Lieutenant Oddie was born at Horsham on 25 September 1879. In 1901 he married Lilian and subsequently joined the staff of the Sheffield *Daily Telegraph* as a journalist. He later became secretary to the Sussex County Cricket Club and lived at 7 Bigwood Avenue. He joined the 28/Middlesex Regiment but was later attached to the 2/Royal Berkshire Regiment. On 23 October 1916 he was killed near Bapaume while leading his platoon into action.

Sergeant Patching was born at Hove in 1874 and was educated at Ellen Street Schools. He had already seen military service and held a medal bestowed in India for the 1897-1898 Tirah Expedition. This was a frontier war against the Alfridi who occupied land near the Khyber Pass. By the time the Great War broke out he was working as a painter and lived at 82 Ellen Street, but he enlisted again in December 1915. He was wounded on the Somme and died of his injuries.

Lance Corporal John Henry Perkins was born

Lieutenant Francis Arthur Joseph Oddie was killed at th[e] Somme on 23 October 1916. (Hove Library)

at Hove in 1897 and educated at Ellen Street Schools. When he enlisted in the 13/Royal Sussex in January 1915 he was living at 38 Payne Avenue. He was wounded on the Somme on 26 October 1916 and died on 4 November 1916.

Private Rees had been a teacher in civilian life. He joined the Prince of Wales Own Civil Service Rifles and was posted as wounded and missing at High Wood.

Second Lieutenant Ross was the only son of Harry Thornton Ross, Superintendent of the Madras Police, and Mrs Ross of 30 Norton Road, and grandson of Major Montagu Battye, Royal Body Guard. He was posted as missing and presumed killed leading his men into battle. His father had already died on 10 March 1914, but his mother Lena Caroline Outram Ross soldiered on until 1934.

Private Stoner was born at Hove in 1891 and educated at Ellen Street Schools. By 1914 he was living at 9 Sheridan Terrace and worked as a milk carrier.

Corporal Wilkinson patriotically volunteered for war service in September 1914 although he was already aged 38 (past the recruiting age at that time), and he was so much older than the other members of his battalion that he was nicknamed 'Pa'. He was educated at Hurstpierpoint College and became a member of the old established firm of Wilkinson, Son & Welch, auctioneers and estate agents, and was in charge of the Hove branch. In 1908 he was Worshipful Master of the Royal Clarence Lodge of Freemasons. His hobby was collecting birds' eggs and he spent holidays on the west coast and islands of Scotland for this purpose. When he enlisted he joined the 20/Royal Fusiliers (Public School Corps). 'He met his death with characteristic devotion. He could easily have ensured his safety. But he saw a man lying wounded and helpless in a crater and he made his way to him to dress his wounds. He had finished this work of mercy and was on the point of returning to his trench when he was struck by a bullet and killed. Thus died a very brave and gallant gentleman.'[9] At the time of his death, it was announced that his brother, Captain T.O. Wilkinson of the 91st Punjabis, currently stationed at Mandalay, Upper Burma, had been ordered to Mesopotamia. It is interesting to note that a Major Augustus Frederick Wilkinson, Indian Army, who died in 1911, is buried in Hove Cemetery.

Hove born Leading Seaman Wyatt was a boatman in civilian life and his parents lived at 18 Sussex Road, right next to Hove seafront. He and his wife lived at 2 Ethel Street.

The family associated with Smithers Brewery has already been mentioned in connection with Captain Smithers who died at Ypres. The Abbeys were also noted brewers affected by the war. The Abbey family acquired the Bristol Brewery, founded by William Hallett, but it did not become known as the Kemp Town Brewery until the 1930s. The Abbeys built up their business and became active in public life. Lieutenant Noël Roland Abbey's grandfather Henry Abbey was Mayor of Brighton in 1875 while his father and his brother John both became High Sheriff of Sussex. John Roland Abbey had a passion for collecting rare books, particularly those with beautiful bindings or fine illustrations. He donated some items to Hove Library while the rest of his collection was sold at Sotheby's in the 1960s for £378,313.

Lieutenant Noël Roland Abbey of the Grenadier Guards was killed in action in 1918. He has three memorial tablets in Sussex and this one is in All Saints Church, Hove. (Author)

Lieutenant Abbey was the second son and was educated at Windlesham House, Brighton, and at Eton, where he won football colours. His family lived at 71 The Drive. He served with the Grenadier Guards and 'fell in the service of his country' on 12 April 1918. 'In this very critical action the Guards held up the German advance for three days suffering severe losses.' These words come from the memorial in All Saints Church, Hove and there is another one in St Andrew's Church, Nuthurst. In the north aisle of Chichester Cathedral there is a memorial tablet beside the gates to a chapel that reads: 'This ancient chapel of St Thomas and St Edmund of Canterbury was restored to use in memory of Noël Roland Abbey', and the rest of the inscription is the same as the one at Hove.

The Vallances too were once connected with the brewery business but Edmund Vallance followed a career in the Army. In 1884 twin children were born at Hove to Edmund Vallance (late of the 19th Hussars) and his wife Jane. The happy event was some consolation because in the previous year their first-born son Vivien died at the age of 6 weeks. The twins were named Valerie and (rather grandly) Vane de Valence Mortimer Vallance. Mortimer was in honour of his mother's maiden name, his grandfather Albert John Mortimer having been the British Paymaster General of the German Legion in Hanover for twenty years. It was not surprising with such a military background that after attending Eton, Vane went to Sandhurst and straight into the 5th (Royal Irish) Lancers in 1904. By 1905 he was a lieutenant and in 1912 he became a captain. A cavalry regiment suited his temperament because he was known as a fearless cross-country rider. He was a popular officer and it is said he was loved by all ranks.

When the Great War broke out the 5th Lancers were stationed at Dublin and went straight to France, being one of the first regiments to be sent across the Channel. They became part of the British Expeditionary Force under Sir John French concentrated near Le Cateau. The Battle of Mons took place in Belgium on 23 August 1914 when the British found themselves up against, and outnumbered by, the crack First German Army. The British held their nerve and fought back with efficient gunfire. Sir John was fully prepared to battle on the next day but found to his disgust that French troops had withdrawn without consultation, leaving his own troops in jeopardy. There was no option but to retreat. The 5th Lancers were the last British troops to leave Mons and the first to re-enter it in November 1918. A youngster from Hove was killed on 2 November 1914 in the retreat from Mons. He was John Edwin May, born in 1896, who lived with his grandfather at 110 Portland Road for eight years because his parents were dead. He spent three years at the training school Mercury (perhaps this was a precursor of TS *Mercury* established in 1913) and then joined the 2/Royal Fusiliers as a boy Bugler in 1912. He was a drummer when he was killed.

Captain Vallance was Mentioned in Despatches twice, on 23 June 1915 and 1 January 1916, and was awarded the Military Cross. He served throughout eleven famous actions, including Mons, the first and second battles of Ypres, and at Le Cateau, the Marne, Aisne, Loos and

Captain Vane de Valence Mortimer Vallance of the 5th (Royal Irish) Lancers survived the Great War. (V. Vallance)

Captain Vallance's Military Cross. In total some forty-two officers from Hove were awarded a Military Cross while fifty-five other ranks were awarded the Military Medal. (V. Vallance)

the Somme. He came through these battles unscathed although it was claimed he had many narrow escapes including the time 'he was in the trench with the 16th Lancers when the sad disaster occurred to that gallant corps'[10]

But he did not enjoy his peaceful existence for long because he died suddenly on 8 July 1924. It is a curious parallel to Arthur Gates and R. Winters of Portslade, who both survived war service only to die in 1925. But in Vane's case it was not illness that carried him off but an accident. He was enjoying a walk along the cliffs at Black Rock when he fell over and crashed onto the beach 80 feet below. Naturally some people wondered if it were a case of suicide, but friends refuted the rumour by saying he had been in a happy frame of mind. It was surely courting danger to venture so close to the edge although he was apparently testing the friable nature of the cliff with his stick as he walked. His daughter Vivien was only 5 years old and never got over the loss of her father whom she could not even remember.

Vane's brother-in-law was Major Roderick Macauly Bertram Needham, who was born in Trinidad in 1880. But like Vane he was a regular soldier and had lived locally since boyhood. Needham served throughout the Boer War and was twice Mentioned in Despatches by Lord Kitchener on 30 July 1902. He was commissioned in the same year. During the Great War he served in France from 9 November 1914 to 13 September 1915 and was sent to Salonika, where he held an important post on the Headquarters Staff of the 26th Division. He was again Mentioned in Despatches on 7 December 1916 and was awarded the Distinguished Service Order in 1918. He returned home safely after war service to his wife and daughters, who were living at 62 Brunswick Place, and finished his military career as a colonel.

The vital work of army chaplains is often overlooked. The Right Reverend Henry Kemble Southwell, who became Bishop of Lewes in 1920, was noted for his 'noble and devoted work organizing the Army chaplains almost from the beginning of war'.[11] He and his wife were not immune from the tragedies of war either as they lost their son, Lieutenant Henry Kenneth Martin Southwell, at sea on 4 June 1919. He was aboard the submarine L-55 on operations in the Baltic Sea when the vessel struck a mine and all thirty-eight members of the crew were killed. But at least the parents had the consolation of a known grave for the bodies were retrieved and buried at Gosport.

The Right Reverend Leonard Hedley Burrows was vicar of Hove and Bishop of Lewes from 1909 to 1914. He was a handsome man and it was a sad day for his many female admirers when he left to become the first Bishop of Sheffield. But he and his wife maintained some ties with

Dr. L. H. Burrows.
Bishop of Lewes & Vicar of Hove.

The Right Reverend Leonard Hedley Burrows was Vicar of All Saints, Hove, and Bishop of Lewes. His son, Second Lieutenant Leonard Righton Burrows, was killed in action in 1915. (Author)

Hove. Their son Leonard Righton Burrows was educated at Charterhouse and was awarded a first class honours degree at Oriel College, Oxford. In November 1912 he set off for Allahabad with Revd W.E.F. Holland to serve in the Educational Missions. When he heard about the war he returned home to volunteer in November 1914 and joined the Northumberland Fusiliers in January 1915. He was a second lieutenant when he was killed in action on 2 October 1915. Mr Lister offered to put his name on Hove's Roll of Honour and his parents were pleased. Louisa wrote: 'Leonard and I would love him mentioned […] Hove Vicarage was his last home on earth.' Another son became a priest, Revd Hedley Robert Burrows.

Captain George Edward Ram was the elder son of Revd Prebendary Robert Digby Ram of St Paul's Cathedral. His mother was Mary, daughter of George Edward Anson CB, a cousin of the Earl of Lichfield. His sister married Sir John Hume-Purves-Hume Campbell of Purves Hall, Berwickshire. Captain Ram went to Trinity Hall, Cambridge, and was a private tutor who lived in The Drive. He joined the 4/Staffordshire Regiment but contracted pneumonia on active service and died at Lady Inchcape's Hospital on 25 March 1916.

Captain Ram of the 4/Staffordshire Regiment died on 25 March 1916. (Hove Library)

Wartime losses afflicted other notable families too. Lieutenant Colonel Spencer Acklom's family had been associated with Hove for many years. His father, Colonel Acklom, and the colonel's wife, lived at 13 Tisbury Road and his grandparents had lived at Hove. Spencer Acklom was born in 1885 and became a professional soldier enlisting in the 72/Highland Light Infantry (Glasgow Highlanders) in 1901. It was stated that he was an expert with the revolver and a boxer of note. When he was stationed in India he won the lightweight championship of All-India at the Lucknow Assault-at-Arms in 1906. At the outbreak of the Great War he was appointed adjutant to the 9/Highland Light Infantry and went to France in November 1914. In July 1916 he was given command of the Northumberland Fusiliers and in the same year was awarded the Military Cross at Richebourg and the Distinguished Service Order at La Boiselle. He was Mentioned in Despatches four times. He was killed in action on 21 March 1918 in the Retreat from Mons.

The Goldie family had strong connections with India. Colonel James Ord Goldie spent the whole of his active career in the sub-continent before retiring to Hove where he lived for a quarter of a century. He was an enthusiastic supporter of the Sussex County Cricket Club and spent many days happily watching cricket. He died aged 78 at 12 Tisbury Road in July 1919. His father and his elder brother, Colonel Barré Goldie, also served in India and the latter retired to Hove and lived in Selborne Road. Colonel James Goldie's son, Major Kenneth Oswald Goldie of the Lancers (Indian Army), saw a considerable amount of service before being appointed military secretary to Lord Willingdon, Governor of Bombay at Madras, a post he still held in 1919. He was awarded the OBE in 1918. Major Goldie's sister was the wife of Lieutenant Colonel Knowles. Colonel James Goldie's other son, Second Lieutenant Barré Herbert Goldie, died in April 1915 while serving with the Indian Army in Egypt.

Judge Martineau, for many years on the Sussex circuit, lost his younger son Major Alfred John Martineau of the Royal Garrison Artillery who was killed in action on 17 April 1917. In civilian life the major had been a throat and ear specialist and surgeon to the relevant hospital at Brighton and lived with his wife in Cambridge Road. Captain J.E. Davidson wrote to Mrs Martineau about the action that cost her husband's life:

> He was forward in an advanced post in a wood recently captured from the enemy, and was shot by a sniper while engaged on observation duty. The bullet passed through his brain and death was instantaneous. Immediately after, the enemy raided the wood making it impossible to recover the major's body until today, when we managed to bring him in after the enemy had retired. Apparently, the enemy carried away his binoculars but, as far as I can tell, all the rest of his private belongings are complete and will be forwarded to you along with his kit.

There were many British light railway systems in operation near the Western Front. (*Illustrated London News* 21 October 1916)

This scene of the Liverpool Irish marching into Lille looks authentic, in contrast to many others that were posed.
(*Illustrated London News* 2 November 1918)

This light railway system was used to convey medical supplies efficiently by trolley to field ambulances near the Front.
(*Illustrated London News* 21 October 1916)

The *Sussex Daily News* (30 April 1917) had this to say: 'At the outbreak of war he was in command at the Fort at Newhaven and proceeded to the Front in April 1916 in charge of a siege battery. He had been associated with the Sussex Garrison Artillery for twelve years and was 44 years of age. An exceedingly keen soldier, and a very able artillerist, he was greatly respected by his officers and men.'

Notes

6. Hove Library Box 2
7. Hove Library Box 1
8. Hove Library Box 3
9. Hove Library Box 5
10. Hove Library Box 6
11. Hove Library Box 4

An on-the-spot drawing of a British 18-pounder in action with Niergnies church in the background.
(*Illustrated London News* 2 November 1918)

CHAPTER 9

Counting the Cost – The Royal Flying Corps and the Royal Naval Air Service

On 13 May 1912 the Royal Flying Corps was established to cover both military and naval aspirations for flying machines. But on 1 July 1914 the Navy decided to go it alone and the Royal Naval Air Service was set up. They remained separate organizations until the Royal Air Force was founded on 1 April 1918.

The government and military authorities did not view the development of reliable aircraft with any sense of urgency and France, Germany and Russia could all muster more aircraft than the British could field. Indeed in 1912 it was claimed there were only nineteen pilots in the entire Royal Flying Corps. Perhaps this was not surprising with the difficulties an aspiring pilot faced. Would he pass the medical and would joining the corps reduce his prospects of promotion? Above all, did he have £75 (later rising to £100) to spare? This was the cost of qualifying for the relevant certificate from the Royal Aero Club. He could only claim reimbursement if and when he was accepted into the flying service.

Once airborne, the major disadvantage of an open cockpit was the extreme cold felt at high altitude. Ice would form on wings and struts and sometimes the compass froze. Airmen smeared their faces with Vaseline to protect them from frostbite or, if that were not to hand, plain engine grease. Meanwhile, the observer was obliged to change delicate glass negatives in his camera with numb fingers, or endeavour to control his pencil while sketching battle positions. Another problem was the difficulty of communication as there were no radios during the first two years of war and when they did come into use the signal only had a range of around 40 miles. Instead, an Aldis lamp could be used to send Morse code messages or sometimes homing pigeons were taken aloft. Then there was the danger of sudden banks of fog or engine malfunction and if a crash were inevitable would it be safer to stay strapped in or risk being thrown out? Once war started friendly fire from allies at the Front became another peril and union flags were painted on the underside of wings to try and prevent such accidents.

At the start of the Great War, the German Fokker was a superior machine but once the Sopwith and Handley Page machines came into operation the balance shifted. The Royal Flying Corps showed its mettle during the Battle of the Somme when almost three hundred bombing raids were carried out, besides hundreds of photographs being taken. But the cost was high with 308 pilots and 171 observers killed, wounded or posted as missing.

One of the earliest squadrons to be formed was Number 1 Squadron Royal Naval Air Service, which came into being on 17 October 1914. To this squadron belonged some eighteen flying aces including Captain George Brian Gates, who was born at Hove on 21 July 1899. Captain Gates was posted to this squadron in 1918, having joined the Royal Naval Air Service on 22 June 1917.

The year 1918 was one of victories for Captain Gates, who was credited with downing fourteen enemy aircraft plus an observation balloon. He flew all his sorties in a British single-seat Sopwith Camel biplane that had only been brought into action on the Western Front in 1917. In

Captain George Brian Gates was awarded the Distinguished Flying Cross.
(Hove Library)

inexperienced hands it was a difficult machine to control but with a good pilot it became a deadly weapon. In fact the Sopwith Camel had more 'kills' than any other British aircraft. Captain Gates was injured in September 1918 but he survived the war.

In November 1918 he was awarded the Distinguished Flying Cross, the award having been instituted on 3 June 1918 for commissioned officers and warrant officers. The following is Captain Gates' citation published in the *London Gazette* (2 November 1918):

> On a recent occasion this officer single-handedly engaged two enemy two-seaters, bringing them both down in flames. He has in addition destroyed a third machine and shot down two kite balloons in flames. On whatever duty engaged – bombing, attacking troops on the ground or fighting in the air – this officer displays consistent courage and skill.

Hot on the heels of this decoration he earned a Bar to add to his DFC. The citation in the *London Gazette* (3 December 1918) read:

> This officer sets a fine example to the other pilots of his squadron being conspicuous for his cool courage and brilliant leadership. During the past month he has accounted for six enemy two-seaters, five driven down in flames, and one crashed.

Another recipient of the Distinguished Flying Cross was Lieutenant Lawrence Arthur Wingfield who was born in 1898 at Richmond, Surrey, but at the outbreak of war was living at 6 San Remo, Kingsway, while his parents lived at 19 Wilbury Avenue. His father George Arthur Wingfield was a London solicitor and Lieutenant Wingfield was an articled clerk to a solicitor. He joined the Inns of Court Officer Training Corps in July 1915, was commissioned into the Royal Fusiliers on 24 August 1915 and at once attached to the 6th Royal Flying Corps.

Lieutenant Lawrence Arthur Wingfield was also a recipient of the Distinguished Flying Cross. He is wearing the uniform of the Royal Flying Corps. (Hove Library)

He inherited a love of flying from his father who founded Shoreham Aerodrome, officially opened on 20 June 1911, as well as the Sussex Aero Club.

At the start of the Battle of the Somme on 1 July 1916, Wingfield successfully bombed and destroyed a railway station. In September his commanding officer wrote to his father:

> I do not know if you heard but the destruction of St Quentin railway station, the scattering for three days of the 71st Prussian Reserve Regiment and the burning of the train loaded with their equipment was his doing. It was a fine piece of work and we are awfully proud of him.

Unfortunately his plane was shot down and he was reported missing. Three weeks were to elapse before it was confirmed he had survived and was a prisoner-of-war. He was taken firstly to Kronach in Bavaria and afterwards to Crefeld. It seemed he had no intention of remaining a prisoner and his father believed he had made previous attempts before his famous escape to Holland in October 1917. His father said he had received a letter from his son containing the statement: 'I have not been able to write regularly for reasons which are good enough but not serious. But if I put them in they would be blacked.'

His escape from Stroken was reported in many newspapers and the *Examiner* (1 January 1918) carried a fascinating account under the headlines 'Airman's Dash for Freedom/Long Tramp from Germany':

> On the night of October 4 he made a dash for liberty. The guard was turned out and bullets whizzed through the air. Wingfield ran into a wire fence and then took a 'header' into a ditch on the other side, which was full of mud and dirty water. For over an hour he remained up to his neck in slush. When all was quiet, he dragged himself out of the ditch, crawled across the road into some long grass, through which he crawled on his hands and knees for perhaps half a mile. It was a very dark night and once clear of the camp he began his long tramp to freedom. By day he lay hidden either in straw, under hedges or in ditches; by night he tramped and tramped, guided entirely by the stars. Several times he entirely lost his bearings and wandered about for hours without knowing in which direction he was going. But always

he managed to find his location again by the stars.

On one particular night, on turning a bend in the road, he was almost run down by two German civilians on bicycles but they called out 'Good night' in German and he replied in his best German with his heart in his mouth. Perhaps they were in a hurry, for they passed on, although Wingfield was still in his British officer's uniform. At length, after 8 miles' tramp through a hostile land, and with very little food, he reached a river on the frontier. By this time he was exhausted and afraid he would never be able to swim across. As luck would have it he stumbled over a wooden plank. Stripping off his clothes he put them on the plank and swam to the other side. The swim, to use his own words, 'bucked him up wonderfully'. When he crossed the river he again lost himself but after wandering about for several hours saw a light in a farmhouse. Creeping up to the window he was delighted to see a man inside the room getting ready for the day's work. He knocked at the door and after telling the farmer and his wife who he was, they gave him food and coffee. Here he had a good wash and rested a little.

By the time Lieutenant Wingfield arrived back in London, he was looking fit and well. In recognition of 'gallantry in escaping from captivity' he was awarded the Military Cross. He survived the war.

Harold Victor Robinson was born in Scotland in 1897 and his father served as a colour sergeant in the Royal Scots during the South African War. His family moved to Hove and Harold attended East Hove Higher Grade School. They lived at 7 Shakespeare Street and young Harold became a motor engineering apprentice. He joined the Territorial Force before the war and was mobilized in August 1914. In November 1914 he contracted bronchial pneumonia and was invalided out of the service. After a long illness and convalescence he succeeded in joining the Royal Naval Air Service as a mechanic and spent the rest of the war serving on airships, flying almost continuously.

In June 1918 the king presented Leading Mechanic Robinson with an Albert Medal in gold. The medal-winning incident took place on 22 December 1917. Five airships stationed at Polegate were ordered to patrol the English Channel and look for U-boats. Each airship carried a crew of three men. They set off early in the morning but they were recalled in the afternoon because of worsening weather conditions. The controller at Polegate considered the snow and fog made it too hazardous for all five to return there and he ordered them to scatter. One landed near Uckfield, two landed near Jevington and two came to earth at Beachy Head. These latter two were recalled to Polegate when visibility improved. Airship Z19 landed safely but airship Z7 clipped airship Z10 and both were enveloped in flames. The bombs on board one airship exploded and the pilot was killed. Robinson and a boy mechanic rushed over to the other one and Robinson managed to extricate the pilot and two crewmen (all severely injured). Then Robinson unclipped the bombs from the burning car and carried them away from the flames. The bomb casing was so hot that he scorched his hands. Hove people were so impressed with his bravery that a collection was organized and £103-8s was raised as a mark of their esteem. At Robinson's own request a gold watch was purchased and suitably inscribed and £80 was put into War Bonds.

Lieutenant Eric Bernard Andrews was born at Hove in 1897. He attended Hove High School and when war broke out he joined Brighton Royal Field Artillery, Territorial Force, straight from school. He obtained his commission in October 1916 and was sent to France in January 1917 and then to Italy after the Austro-German offensive in that country. He later returned to England and joined the air service in February 1918 and then served on the Western Front. On 16 September 1918 his plane flew beyond German lines and did not return. He was posted missing and it was hoped he had been taken prisoner. A member of his squadron wrote to his parents: 'He was with a very good pilot and he himself being a particularly good observer, I can scarcely imagine that they would come to grief in ordinary combat with the enemy.'

Meanwhile his parents remained on tenterhooks until his death was reported in December 1918. His commander wrote: 'He was one of our very best observers and a great loss to the squadron.' His elder brother Private William Frederick Andrews joined the 2/Royal Sussex in December 1915 and died on 7 August 1917 of colitis on active service in Waziristan, on the north-west frontier of India. Their parents lived at 2 Osmond Gardens.

Captain Jack Henry Woolf Barnato was born on 7 June 1894 and his first name was Isaac but he preferred to be called Jack. Name changing ran in the family because his father Barney Barnato's birth name was Barnett Isaacs. Barney Barnato was born in Petticoat Lane, London, and he and his brother Henry were educated at the Jews' Free School in Bell Lane, leaving at the age of 14. The fortunes of the Barnato brothers was a true case of rags to riches because their father was a dealer in second-hand clothing while they headed for South Africa to join the diamond rush. They worked very hard and eventually built up a massive business diamond-dealing in Kimberley. In fact the Barnato Company became such a success Cecil Rhodes feared it might threaten his imperial ambitions. Instead in 1888 Rhodes bought out the company for a sum in the region of £5,000,000. Jack was also there for a while, along with two other young Barnatos, helping to consolidate their fortunes.

Unlike his predecessors, Captain Barnato received a good education, starting off at Windlesham House, Brighton, before going to Charterhouse and finishing with Trinity Hall, Cambridge. He was so keen to enlist in 1914 that he spent a year in the ranks as a private with the Royal Fusiliers before joining the Royal Naval Air Service in 1915. He became a pioneer too because he flew in one of the earliest episodes of waging war from the air. He was one of the first four airmen to bomb Constantinople and Adrianople in April 1916, for which feat he was Mentioned in Despatches. On 13 October 1917 he married Dorothy, the only child of Mr and Mrs Joe Lewis of South Africa. His bride was very young and the marriage was brief. In October 1918 the captain caught influenza and within a few days the illness developed into septic pneumonia. He was aged 24 when he died on 20 October at Duke Street Mansions, Grosvenor Square, London. He was buried in Willesden Jewish Cemetery. His widow was aged 18. His mother, the widow of Barney Barnato, lived at 4 Adelaide Mansions, Hove, and Captain Barnato often stayed there but he also had a home at Furze Mount, Upper Colwyn Bay, North Wales. Captain Barnato left £661,000. His younger brother Woolf Barnato served with the British forces in Palestine.

Sergeant Frank Bernard Brown was born at Hove in 1898, educated at George Street Schools, and was a brass furnisher by trade. He enlisted on 24 August 1914 but was killed on 3 August 1918 at Yatesbury, Wiltshire, while flying a DH6 machine by 'running into a hill during a mist'. The DH6 was a biplane designed by Geoffrey de

Havilland and used for training new recruits of the Royal Flying Corps. It was generally regarded as a safe machine and the single cockpit contained basketwork seats for instructor and trainee.

Flight Lieutenant Charles Hamilton Murray Chapman was born in 1892 and educated at Monmouth Grammar School and Manchester University. When war broke out he offered his services to the Navy because he had some knowledge of wireless telegraphy. He became a wireless operator aboard one of the ships that took part in the action under Admiral Hood off the Belgian coast in October 1914. Later he transferred to a minesweeping trawler and spent the first winter of the war on duty in the North Sea. On one occasion his ship undertook a week of voluntary service in a heavily mined area. In June 1915 he obtained a commission in the Royal Naval Air Service and in September of the same year was sent with a squadron to France. He received severe injuries in an accident when his aircraft developed engine trouble and he needed six months to recuperate. On 22 March 1916 he married Olive Simpson and for fourteen months undertook valuable work as an instructor at a home air station. 'He loved this job and was never so happy as when exploring the wonders of cloudland.' [12] He was accidentally killed on 23 February 1918. His obituary stated: 'His bright and vivid personality endeared him to all. A great lover of nature, he was a keen student of all matters relating to science and natural history, and a story book for children on the subject, written and illustrated by himself, is to be published.' His parents lived at Hove.

Lieutenant Stephen James Chapman was born in Byron Street in 1891 and was educated at East Hove Schools. He became an engineer. At the outbreak of war he was on a visit to his sister who lived in Canada. He joined the Army in January 1915 and was a dispatch rider before transferring to the Royal Flying Corps. On 5 March 1918 he married by special licence Léonié, an only child and the granddaughter of Major William Percy, Military Knight of Windsor. The lieutenant was an only son and on 6 June 1918 he was killed in an aeroplane collision at Littlestone-on-Sea, New Romney, Kent.

Lieutenant Stephen James Chapman was killed in an air collision over Kent on 6 June 1918. (Hove Library)

Lieutenant Charles Chrimes RAF was stationed in Malta in 1918. He was awarded the Italian La Croce al Merito de Guerra and a commemorative medal for his service in Liberia. A newspaper report stated: 'After their return Lieutenant Chrimes and his second pilot were feted at the expense of the Italian Government.' Reference was made to 'the way these British aviators had achieved their task in the face of the most determined opposition on the part of the enemy'. Then Lieutenant Chrimes took the salute as 5,000 troops marched past.

Second Lieutenant William Martin Vernon Cotton was born at Exeter in 1892. He was educated at Brighton Grammar School and Shoreham Grammar School. He later settled in Canada and earned a living as a bank clerk. In 1914 he enlisted in the Canadian Expeditionary Force and in 1916 was commissioned to the Royal Flying Corps. He served as an observer and was shot down on 21 December 1916. A handwritten note on his record card states 'His machine was brought down behind the German lines in Flanders.'

Second Lieutenant Hubert Lyon Bingham Crabbe was born in County Limerick, Ireland and his father was Major A. Bingham Crabbe of the 8th Hussars. Crabbe was educated at Marlborough and joined the 3rd Hussars but was attached to the Royal Flying Corps on 5 January 1917. He went missing on 15 May 1918 and was presumably killed in action. There is a terse note on his record card: 'no trace, flying.' When Hove's Roll of Honour was printed in 1920, he was listed under 'Missing – Presumed Dead'.

Flight Lieutenant Alfred Richard Creese's home address was 41 Langdale Gardens but he was an Oxford scholar when he joined the air service in 1917. He saw active service in Italy from April to September 1918 but after contracting influenza and pneumonia he died in Cliff Military Hospital on 13 November 1918.

Second Air Mechanic Ernest Crewe was born in St John's Road, Hove, and was still there in 1914 running a business as a motor car proprietor at numbers 8-10 on 29 March 1917 when he joined the Royal Flying Corps. But his days of service were short because he contracted pneumonia after working in very bad weather and died on 11 April 1917 at Farnborough Military Hospital. He left a widow and three young children.

Lieutenant Ernest James Garner was born at Hove in 1893 and educated at Portland Road and Connaught Road Schools. He lived at 50

Cowper Street and was a motor mechanic by trade. He enlisted in the Royal Naval Air Service on 9 September 1914 as an air mechanic 1st grade. At some stage of the war he was rescued from the North Sea and taken to a prisoner-of-war camp in Holland from where he was released on 2 September 1917. He was Mentioned in Despatches and awarded the Air Force Cross for consistent good patrol work and bombing work from 1 April 1918 to 30 October 1918. He survived the war.

Second Lieutenant Derrick Sivewright Johnson was born in 1895 in Cape Town. He attended Brighton College and the family lived at Melrose House, Wilbury Road. He enlisted in August 1914 but died on 4 December 1916 in 'aerial fight', although in the confusion of the times he was first officially reported to have died whilst a prisoner-of-war. His father was Lieutenant Colonel Frank Johnson.

Lieutenant Derrick Sivewright Johnson was killed in action on 4 December 1916. (Hove Library)

Captain Harold Julian Miles was born at Hove and educated at Brighton Grammar School. He lived at 70 St Leonard's Road and earned a living as a chemist. He joined the flying service on 26 August 1914 and was awarded the Croix de Guerre avec Palme for distinguished flying during the time the French Army was in difficulties, the honour being bestowed upon him in November 1918. It was claimed that he was the first pilot to fly from England to Ireland at night, his route taking him from Andover to Dublin, via Bristol and Wrexford, with the return flight via Holyhead, Liverpool and Swindon. He survived the war.

Lieutenant Alfred George Bathurst Norman was born in 1898 and educated at Wick School, Hove, and Harrow. He lived at 10 Palmeira Square and joined the Royal Flying Corps as a cadet in April 1917. After a course in night flying and bombing at Salisbury, he joined the Independent Force in France in June 1918 and was in Paris on duty during the Armistice celebrations. On 20 November 1918 he was killed instantly when his plane crashed in fog near Amiens. He was the author of a book of poems entitled *Ditchling Beacon* in which his love of Sussex was evident. It was stated that 'his poems have a real originality because they were the spontaneous outcome of his own deepest feelings'. [13] His father was Revd Harry Bathurst Norman.

The Thorowgoods were living in London when war was declared but when their only son decided to enlist his parents moved to Hove, first buying a house in Sackville Gardens and later moving to 25 Rutland Gardens. Captain Leslie Vernon Thorowgood (handwritten note 'Flight Commander') was killed in a flying accident at Lakedown on 22 March 1918.

Air Mechanic Arnold Walker was born in 1893 in Surrey but had lived at Hove since 1895 and was educated at Connaught Road Schools. He enlisted in the Royal Flying Corps in October 1914 and became an observer. He was Mentioned in Despatches and Major Lewis put Walker's name forward for promotion. But before that could happen he was killed in action on 30 March 1916 in an aerial battle over Bapaume when his plane was shot down over German lines. 'First they thought his machine was only missing, the next day the Germans dropped a message saying he was killed.' [14] This gentlemanly behaviour

In 1918 Captain Prince Albert (later George VI), accompanied by Major Greig flew to France. Their regulation flying kit designed to keep out the cold looks extraordinary. (Illustrated London News 2 November 1918)

by German aviators was not uncommon in the early part of the war, indeed there seemed to be a kind of chivalry between air combatants on both sides. The Germans buried Walker and marked his grave and his own squadron found it a year later.

It is interesting to note that it was the celebrated German pilot Lieutenant Max Immelmann who shot down Walker's plane. Immelmann was an effective fighter who surprised his enemy with an attack from beneath, followed by a steep climb to attack the British pilot from a point where his view was obstructed by his own wings. Immelmann was the recipient of the rare Pour le Mérite medal, which was nicknamed the Blue Max in his honour. He was also awarded the Iron Cross. Like many aviators he was superstitious and liked to have a lucky clover-leaf about his person, which his mother had given him. A pilot of the Royal Flying Corps shot down Immelmann's plane on 18 June 1916 and he was killed.

Signalman Frederick George Victor Young lived at 41 Coleridge Street and joined the Royal Naval Volunteer Reserve in August 1914. In January 1915 he was invalided out of the service with bronchitis. When he recovered he joined the Royal Flying Corps in May of that year. He became a wireless operator and saw service at the Somme. While in France he went down with pneumonia and was invalided out for the second time in March 1917. He was sent to recover in the sanatorium at Foredown in Portslade. He was due for discharge when he caught the dreaded influenza followed by pneumonia and died at the age of 30 on 23 October 1918.

Notes

12. Hove Library Box 1
13. Hove Library Box 3
14. Hove Library Box 5

CHAPTER 10

Afterwards

At 11.00 am on 11 November 1918 the carillon of bells in Hove Town Hall 'rang out its joyous peal'[15] and people rushed from all sides to read a copy of the Prime Minister's message displayed outside, declaring the Armistice. Then the Mayor of Hove appeared on the steps to make a speech. 'Those who were present will not forget the figure of the Vicar of Hove as he stood in full view of the throng waving a huge Union Jack.'[15]

In the afternoon two airmen astonished the inhabitants, 'by their thrilling feats and the discharge of coloured lights. Looping the loop appeared to be mere child's play to them […] Their sudden nose dives made earth-crawlers hold their breath, and the next instant they were "climbing" with extraordinary rapidity into the clouds. Such a superb display of flying had seldom been seen over the town.'[16]

That evening every church in Hove flung wide its doors and people poured in. At All Saints every part of the huge church was packed including the Lady Chapel and the organ chamber. It was felt that the day was also one for solemn remembrance and there was no dancing in the streets and 'no rowdiness in or in front of public houses'.

The official celebration to mark the signing of the peace treaty was set for 19 July 1919 and honoured throughout the country and the empire. At Hove some 1,500 ex-servicemen from all the different battlefronts assembled on Brunswick Lawns. They marched in a long column to Hove Town Hall, where they paused to salute the two large wreaths placed at the entrance, while the band of the 2nd Highland Light Infantry played *For all the Saints.* The march then resumed to the

Goldstone football ground where an afternoon of sports had been laid on. Unfortunately, by then the persistent drizzle had turned into a downpour. Despite the bad weather thousands of people ventured to the Lawns that evening to watch the lighting of surplus Admiralty flares placed along the seawall and the brilliant illumination that followed. Schoolchildren had better luck with the weather for their own celebrations at Hove Recreation Ground on 30 July while the weather was of no concern for the tea and entertainment put on at Hove Town Hall on 1 August for the mothers, widows and children of the fallen. Lastly, at the express wish of ex-servicemen, a service was held at All Saints 'to the memory of our dead comrades'.

'The idea that Hove is peopled mainly by millionaires is a picturesque delusion', wrote H.M. Walbrook in 1920. Even so the town's efforts to raise money for war funds were extraordinary, although the mayor grumbled too many people wanted to hold flag-days at Hove. The money recorded as passing through the accounts of Hove War Savings Committee came to over £2,500,000, and this was claimed to be but a small proportion because many residents preferred to invest through their usual London banks and stockbrokers.

For England's Flag Day in May 1916 Mrs Buhl and Miss Vera Starkey, plus helpers, set up their stall on Kingsway at the foot of Westbourne Villas. The little boy in his miniature car was Master Wills of Westbourne Terrace. (D. d'Enno)

The tank nicknamed Egbert made an eye-catching centrepiece for fund collecting in July 1918 on behalf of War Weapons Week. (Author)

Fundraising was encouraged by imaginative events such as the arrival of the tank dubbed Egbert on the boundary between Hove and Brighton in July 1918. It remained there for three days and attracted vast crowds of people. At times Egbert would trundle across Brunswick Lawns and surmount a pile of sandbags to demonstrate what it could do.

In recognition of Hove's sterling work, the town was awarded its own tank as a war relic. The tank was called Hova and arrived straight from France on 23 September 1919. It was a mark IV female tank number 2591 and was 30 feet in length and 9 feet 4 inches in height. When in action the tank was armed with six Lewis guns and 24,000 rounds of small arms ammunition, and its crew consisted of one officer, one sergeant and six men.

The tank, manned by a crew under Lieutenant A.R. Roberts MC, left the railway depot in Sackville Road 'grim and battle-scarred in appearance, flying the Union Jack and the Tank Corps colours', [17] and proceeded to Hove Park. Captain W.F. Farrar MC, who had actually fought inside the tank, presented it to the town. He gave a speech in which he said he knew some people did not want these relics with their constant reminder of slaughter in public parks but they were a symbol of British ingenuity, resource and pluck and had saved many British lives. Hova stood just inside the south-west gate of Hove Park and lasted until around 1937 when it was disposed off for scrap metal.

Sir Edwin Lutyens (1869-1944) designed his only Sussex war memorial for Hove. His name has become synonymous with war memorials and the Cenotaph in Whitehall is perhaps his best-known work. Other impressive monuments are the Memorial at Thiepval and the one at Etaples, Pas de Calais. These are huge in size when compared with Hove's modest memorial, which cost £1,537.

The circular column is 20 feet in height and made of granite, like the plinth, while a bronze figure of St George stands on top. Sir George Frampton (1860-1928) sculpted the figure. He produced the Edith Cavell memorial in London in 1920. He was also responsible for the famous figure of Peter Pan in Kensington Gardens. On the south side of Hove's memorial 'Their Name Liveth for Evermore' is inscribed. Rudyard Kipling took the phrase from Ecclesiasticus and suggested it

Hove was so diligent in generating funds for the war effort that the town was awarded a British tank as a war souvenir. Here it is arriving at Hove Park where it rusted for the next eighteen years or so. (From Hove in the Great War)

to Lutyens as suitable for memorials. There was no space for names and these were inscribed on brass tablets and installed in the vestibule of Hove Library.

Lutyens designed two other war memorials similar to the one at Hove. They are at Mells, Somerset, and Fordham, Cambridgeshire.

Like Sir Arthur Conan Doyle, Lutyens too suffered loss in the Great War when five nephews died. Charles Lutyens was killed at Gallipoli in 1915, Cyril and another Charles died near Ypres in 1917, and Lionel and Derek were killed in 1918.

It is pleasant to record that the commissioning and execution of the work for Hove went ahead smoothly in contrast to other Lutyens memorials dotted around the country where local disputes delayed completion for years. The Hove memorial was one of the first to be unveiled with Lord Leconfield, Lord Lieutenant of Sussex, performing the ceremony on 27 February 1921. (Lutyens was unable to attend because he was in India.) As the flags fluttered to the ground, four young buglers sounded the Last Post and the sun highlighted St George. A nearby enclosure was reserved for 1,000 bereaved relatives.

When Hove's War Memorial was instituted, Grand Avenue was a quiet and spacious road. Nowadays when Remembrance Sunday comes around, police have to block both ends of Grand Avenue. (Author)

The base of the memorial was soon covered with floral tributes. Perhaps the most touching was a faded bunch of violets with the message 'From the little baby who he never saw'. The Mayor of Hove and councillors provided a large wreath of laurel and arum lilies while the tribute from Brighton & Hove Albion Football Club bore the message 'Their last and Finest Goal'. The club lost four players – Jasper (Ginger) Batey, Charlie Dexter, Charlie Matthews and Robert Whiting, plus Fred Bates, groundsman.

Jasper Matthews Batey was a professional football player who was born at South Shields on 7 July 1891. He joined Brighton & Hove Albion for the 1913-1914 season and played half-back but by the

Sir Edwin Lutyens designed Hove's War Memorial and it was unveiled on 27 February 1921. (Author)

following season was playing left-half. He was a popular figure with the public and lived at 9 Leighton Road. On 4 January 1915 he enlisted as a private in the Army Cyclist Corps and served as a messenger. He was killed in action on 23 October 1916.

Charlie Dexter was born in Derby in 1889, the third son of the family and there was a sister called Dolly. Although he was a 'cricketer of no mean order' he became a professional footballer in 1911 and he played for Sheffield Wednesday before joining Brighton & Hove Albion in 1914. He lived at 6 Montgomery Street. He played half-back and his career was taking off well at the Goldstone when war broke out. He enlisted in the Sportsman's Battalion 17/Middlesex Regiment in November 1914. After training he spent around six months in France and then, according to a handwritten note on his service card, was 'invalided home with septic poisoning probably through being gassed'. He was in hospital at Torquay for several months before being moved to Exeter where he received his discharge from the Army on 10 April 1916. He returned home to Derby in failing health and died peacefully there on 27 June 1916. He was aged 27. He was buried at Derby and one mourner at his funeral was Miss E. Holland, his fiancée.

Charlie Matthews was born on 27 January 1889 at Falmer and given the Christian names Clement Henry, but perhaps he did not like them as he was always known as Charlie. He was educated at Horsham and became a professional footballer by playing for Horsham. He was also a bricklayer. On 23 February 1911 he joined the Territorial Force 4/Royal Sussex Regiment and in December of the same year he joined Brighton & Hove Albion where he played half-back. Although he made twelve appearances for the club, he only ever scored one goal. He was killed in action on 15 August 1915 at Suvla Bay during the Gallipoli campaign when a Turkish sniper shot him. He held the 1915 star and service medal.

Private Clement Henry Matthews (photographed in his Brighton & Hove Albion football shirt) was killed at Gallipoli on 15 August 1915. (Hove Library)

Bob Whiting, a professional footballer, was born in West Ham on 6 January 1883 and while he was with the Albion he lived with his family at 9 Coleridge Street. For reasons unknown the sporting fraternity nicknamed him Pom-Pom. He joined the Sportsman's Battalion/Middlesex Regiment on 1 January 1915 but was killed in action in France on 28 April 1917. He left a widow and three children, the youngest a 3-month old baby born while he was at the Front and whom he had never seen. Perhaps it was his widow who placed the bunch of violets at the war memorial. A vicious rumour concerning his death was reported in the *Sussex Daily News* (3 September 1919):

> For some time past a dastardly rumour has been in circulation in Brighton to the effect that Whiting, who greatly distinguished himself as goalkeeper in the service of Brighton & Hove Albion, and previously with Chelsea, was shot as a deserter in France, the real fact being that he fell gallantly in action. Unhappily the rumour has now reached the ears of his widow, and has come as a great shock.

Mrs Whiting took immediate action by forwarding to Albert Underwood, Albion's secretary, precious official documents and letters, 'which dispute a foul calumny'. She requested maximum publicity. In fact Whiting was killed by shellfire while attending the wounded.

There was no public war memorial at Portslade until twelve years

Portslade's War Memorial is situated in peaceful surroundings. This was how it looked in the 1950s. (Author)

after the war ended although the churches of St Nicolas and St Andrew had already instituted their own memorials. The war memorial was unveiled in 1930 outside the Royal British Legion Hall in Trafalgar Road, Portslade. It was not the best place to remember the fallen on 11 November because of the traffic and in 1954 was removed to the more tranquil surroundings of Easthill Park, which opened in 1948. At first there were some modest flower beds in front of the memorial but since then the site has been re-designed with paving, formal flowerbeds and dignity has been added by a fine planting of trees.

Today, judicious planting has enhanced the memorial's surroundings. (Author)

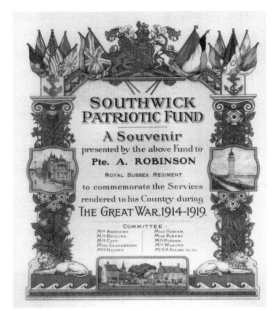

Fishersgate was once reckoned as part of the parish of St Andrew's, Portslade. Private A. Robinson lived in Fishersgate and when he returned from war, a grateful council presented him with this magnificent certificate.
(N. Sharp)

The British Legion came to the rescue of a Portslade widow. In March 1925 Mr Todd died, having been gassed during the war. He left a widow and five children, the youngest being a 1-year old. For six terrible weeks no money came into the house although neighbours and friends rallied around as best they could. The British Legion fought her case, ensuring she received a widow's war pension of ten shillings a week.

John William Lister (1870-1951) was aged 22 when he was appointed Hove's first Chief Librarian at a salary of £70 a year. It was a popular choice and six years later the *Hove Gazette* commented: 'A more tactful and obliging librarian than Mr Lister it would be hard to find. May his shadow never grow less!' But his first few years at Hove were unhappy and indeed Lister himself described them as 'sixteen years of purgatory'. This was because of the cramped and unsuitable surroundings first in Grand Avenue and then in Third Avenue before the move to the beautiful and spacious new building in Church Road in 1908. On the other hand he liked to emphasize that he came to Hove as a delicate boy but thanks to the splendid air he had never had a week on sick leave during his forty-three years as Chief Librarian. He was married twice, his first wife having died in 1921. His second wife was Eva Jean Farnol, chief assistant at Hove Library, and a cousin of the famous author Jeffrey Farnol. After the Great War Lister set about obtaining as much information as possible concerning the men with Hove associations who had died in the conflict. He had specially printed cards produced with the Hove coat of arms and the heading Municipal War Record, Roll of Honour and despatched them to the relevant families. It is because of his tireless work that so many illuminating details have come down to us.

Most families were honoured and proud to be asked to contribute and they were anxious that the sacrifice their men had made should not be forgotten. It gave them some comfort. But there were others who were bitter.

For example, Mrs Minnie Smith wrote from 78 Westbourne Street about her son who in more peaceful times earned a living as a steward at Hove Club in Fourth Avenue:

> My dear son was a splendid fellow, and was twice rejected as medically unfit at Chichester but was called, at Hove, when they were very short of men, and passed the third time [...] It has been a sad blow to me, the light of my life has gone out because they passed him and he was quite unfit and his last words to me when he went were "Mother, whatever I go through I will stick it to the last."

He enlisted on 15 June 1917 and was sent to Italy in November. He contracted measles and was very ill and afterwards constantly had dysentery until he was taken ill suddenly and died of double pneumonia on 18 May 1918. He had two brothers also serving in the armed forces, one a second lieutenant in the RAF and the other at Salonika.

Private George Burchell was born at Hove on 22 November 1893. He became a butcher and lived at 45 Wordsworth Street. He enlisted on 3 September 1914 in the 7/Royal Sussex Regiment but died on 10 November 1916. His brother, Sergeant Henry William Burchell, also of the Royal Sussex Regiment, suffered a head injury in France in October 1915 that blew away part of his skull and blinded him in one eye. He was discharged as medically unfit, suffering from severe headaches and epilepsy, and was awarded a pension of eighteen shillings and nine pence a week. But then the authorities decided to slash his pension to twelve shillings and sixpence. He could not manage financially on such a pittance and was obliged to seek work on transport at Newhaven. He died in his sleep from an epileptic fit. His father was also wounded in the war and two other brothers served as well.

Trimmer William Henry Hughes was born in 1877. He lived at 3 Conway Place and earned a living as a gas labourer. He was a member of the Royal Naval Reserve and in 1917 served on the training ship HMS *Ganges*. By 1919 he was aboard the minesweeper *Queen of the North* when he drowned in the North Sea on 20 July. On hearing the sad news, his mother went insane and had to be confined to Hellingly Asylum.

Private Albert Edward Wheeler of the Middlesex Regiment lived at 8 St Leonard's Road and in civilian life worked as a motor driver. He saw a great deal of action at the Western Front, the Somme and Delville Wood where he was severely wounded. On 19 October 1917 he was discharged as medically unfit and received a full pension. But he did not survive long and died at home on 6 November the same year. 'His brother Claude Fogo Wheeler, died as a result of marching to Chichester where he was rejected from military service.'[18] Their father was a Crimean War veteran who served as a trooper with the 6th (Inniskillin) Dragoons.

One family could not forgive the fact their son Private William Rowland of the Royal Sussex never came home on leave. He enlisted in September 1914, leaving behind his home at 63 Wordsworth Street and his trade as a butcher. He served for three years and three months on the Eastern Front and was in Palestine before being sent to France. Two months later he was killed in action on 29 July 1918.

But some men were desperate to be part of the action despite rejection. Second Lieutenant Robert Moore was educated at Sherborne and lived at 38 Cromwell Road, earning a living as a bank clerk. He suffered a number of rejections because of his eyesight but eventually joined the Public Schools Corps (19th Royal Fusiliers) in September 1914 as a private. He served at the Front and received his commission in July 1916, transferring to the Rifle Brigade. On 14 August 1917 at Steenbrek, in front of Langermark, he was wounded early in the action but refused to leave his men. He gallantly led his company into action, killing four Germans before being struck down by machine-gunfire and rifle fire. He died from his wounds the following day.

Other men came home still suffering from the effects of war, particularly gas poisoning. Lance Corporal James Archibald Parker of the Royal Engineers, who was a carpenter before enlisting in November 1914, died at Hove from the effects of chlorine gas on 11 March 1917. Another man also died of gas poisoning but not at the hand of the enemy. He was Private Alan Bernard who was privately educated at Hove High School and lived at 61 Carlisle Road. He was a surveyor's pupil when he joined the Royal Sussex in October 1916. He died on 20 January 1917 at Newhaven. It sounds as though it was a tragic training accident.

There were other sad cases where men never recovered from shell shock. Alderman Barnett Marks was Mayor of Hove for three years. His son Arthur Sampson Marks was born at Hove in 1885 and educated at Brighton Grammar School. He enlisted in October 1914 in the 9/Royal Sussex and was sent to France in 1915. 'For a year or so he served with a trench mortar battery until invalided home with severe shell shock. He was in various hospitals for another twelve months when he was finally discharged with the honorary rank of lieutenant.'[19] He was given an appointment on the War Savings Committee. He died in London on 25 October 1918 of pneumonia after an illness lasting just two days. His body was brought back to Brighton by train accompanied by relatives and he was buried in the Jewish Cemetery at Brighton, the ceremony being conducted by Revd B.B. Lieberman, minister of the synagogue. There were many floral tributes including wreaths from the Sussex Masonic Club and the Sussex Motor Yacht Club.

Other men never returned home because they died as prisoners of war. Private George Humphrey was born at Brighton in 1880 but by 1914 lived at 20 Payne Avenue. He worked as an ice porter for the Ice Company in Holland Road for eight years. He enlisted in June 1916 in 2/5 Manchester Regiment but then his wife became ill and he was given six months' exemption. He rejoined and during the one year and five days he served, he was wounded three times. On 1 March 1918 he was taken prisoner and died on 9 October 1918 when he fell out while on a march and perished at the roadside of starvation at St Remy, France. He left a widow and two sons.

Gunner David Henry Blanch was born at Hove in 1899 and educated at George Street Schools. He lived at 96 Montgomery Street and was a market gardener. In September 1915 he enlisted in the Royal Garrison Artillery and died on 29 August 1918 as a prisoner-of-war in France.

Several men, weakened by their wartime service, succumbed to the dreaded influenza. One such was Trooper John William David Ansell who died at the home he shared with his wife at 10 Alpine Road on 6 November 1918. His mother lived at 69 Tamworth Road. He had also been wounded. Trooper Ansell was born at Woolwich in 1879 but the family moved to Hove where he was educated at Ellen Street Schools. He worked as a brick-maker before enlisting with the 11th Hussars in 1896. He held the South African Medal and the Mons Star. His brother Private David Irvin Ansell was born at Hove in 1891, educated at Portland Road Schools and worked as a box-maker. He joined the 1/Suffolk Regiment in April 1916 and died on 6 October 1918 from malaria at Salonika.

The much decorated army veteran Major Douglas Drysdale Rose came back to Hove with most of his left hand missing, and had suffered nine wounds. He was awarded the Military Cross, the Croix de Chevalier de la Légion d'Honneur, the Croix de Guerre and was Mentioned in Despatches. He was born in 1884 in London, educated at Wellington and enlisted in the Royal Sussex Militia (Artillery) in 1901. He was commissioned to the Royal Field Artillery in 1903 and he also held the South African Medal. He lived at 2 St Aubyns.

Portslade-born John Frederick William Banfield of the Machine Gun Corps returned home from the Western Front with his left eye missing, no feeling on that side of his face and an injured right hip. He received his injuries during the run-up to the Battle of Arras. On 19 March 1917 Banfield was busy with the rest of the No. 1 Machine-Gun crew firing their Lewis gun at a nearby copse. In the noise and confusion of battle, some soldiers retreated but he remained at his post. A German biplane flew overhead making three complete circuits of Banfield's position while he desperately tried to fix the aircraft in his sights but the angle was wrong. The German leant over the side of his plane and lobbed a bomb, hitting the ammunition next to Banfield and blowing it up.

Banfield endured thrity-six operations over the years, but the surgeons managed to fuse his hip and eventually he could walk again. He was given a glass eye that he sometimes forgot to insert, but the socket continued to bleed at times. This was not surprising because, when he was aged 69, surgeons created a new eye socket for him, and afterwards showed him a kidney-dish full of shrapnel extracted during the process.

A few men were lucky enough to have a 'good' war. For instance, there was Harold Harris, manager of Lloyd's Bank, Palmeira Branch, Gwydyr Mansions. He continued with his bank work until enlisting in May 1916. He became a sergeant in 7/Tank Battalion. The first six months were spent in Belgium 'where the tanks were hardly a success on account of the mud'.[20] He was present at the Somme and both battles of Cambrai in 1917 and 1918 and on 29 September he was awarded the Distinguished Conduct Medal for his services in crossing the Canal du Nord, clearing away barbed wire for the infantry and attacking Bourlon Village. 'Fortune favoured me and I came home in perfect health.'[20] In fact it was in the nature of a miracle because those early tanks were notoriously unreliable and easily became death traps. The gallant sergeant even offered to drive the tank Hova from Hove Station if the authorities wished a Hove resident to perform the task, but his offer was not taken up.

The Press stated that Major Frederick Stewart Modera DSO & Bar MC, 'had a wonderful war career'. He was born in Lancashire in 1887 and came to Hove as a child where his parents lived at Wilbury Lodge, Wilbury Road. He was the great-grandson of Major William Alexander Riach of the 79th Cameron Highlanders, who had served in the Peninsular and Waterloo campaigns. Modera was educated at Hove and at Charterhouse and afterwards at University College, Oxford, where he gained an honours degree in jurisprudence. He became a barrister-at-law at the Inner Temple in London. He married Mary Antonetta Rolland on 21 January 1915 and they had two daughters. He enlisted in September 1914 as a private in the Royal Fusiliers. Within two years he had risen to be second-in-command of a Service Battalion (3rd Public Schools Battalion/Royal Fusiliers). He was Mentioned in Despatches in June 1917, was awarded the Military Cross for his actions at High Wood on 20 July 1916 and received the Distinguished Service Order and Bar for the Vieux Berquin action of 12/13 April 1918. He was slightly wounded on 28 September 1918 but survived the war.

Another unscathed warrior was Captain Adrian Wrigley Fosbrooke-Hobbes of the Royal Horse Artillery who was born at Sutton Coldfield in 1896 and educated at Brighton Grammar School. His parents lived at 54 Sackville Gardens and his father was a doctor. He served in France from May 1915 to November 1915, in Mesopotamia from December 1915 to June 1916. A spell in India followed and he was in

Palestine and Syria from November 1917 to June 1919. His Military Cross was bestowed on him on 14 July 1918 in the Jordan Valley, Palestine, for galloping across the open under heavy fire, directing the fire of the battery on a counter-attack of Turks and Germans and with two others capturing six officers, 120 men and twelve machine-guns. His brother, Captain Alan J. Fosbrooke-Hobbes served in the Tank Corps in France and returned home too. Another brother, Johnston Fosbrooke-Hobbes was in South Africa.

Sergeant James Henry Heath was fortunate as well. He was born in 1874 and educated at Ellen Street Schools. He became a general labourer and lived with his wife at 92 Clarendon Road. He enlisted in the 18/Middlesex Regiment (Pioneers) and was sent to France the following November. He served throughout the battles of the Somme, Arras, Nieuport and Ypres and also during the last big push. In April 1918 he was awarded the Distinguished Conduct Medal: 'For conspicuous gallantry and devotion to duty and consistent good work during a long period. He has maintained a high standard of discipline and efficiency among his men, and has always shown great skill and

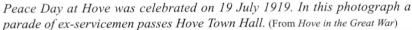

Peace Day at Hove was celebrated on 19 July 1919. In this photograph a parade of ex-servicemen passes Hove Town Hall. (From *Hove in the Great War*)

determination at his work.' After all this activity he ended up in hospital with lumbago and was demobbed on 7 March 1919.

If it had not been for Mr Lister, we should not know the sad story of Private Archibald Holland who lived at 88 Cowper Street and worked as a shop assistant. He enlisted with the Royal Sussex Regiment in 1914 and died in France on 9 October 1917. A handwritten note on his service card states: 'He was found in the country by Mrs Holland's son and was being ill-used; they brought him home with them and Mrs Wood brought him up. Nothing was known about his birth or his parents.'

Notes

15. Walbrook, op. cit.
16. Sussex Daily News, 12 November 1916
17. Walbrook, op. cit.
18. Hove Library Box 6
19. Hove Library Box 3
20. Hove Library Box 6

Bibliography

Archives

At Hove Library in connection with the Roll of Honour engraved on brass tablets in the vestibule, there are six box files containing Hove Library War Records as follows:

Box 1 A – DA
Box 2 DE – HI
Box 3 HO – PA
Box 4 PE – V
Box 5 Dead W – Z Missing A – Z Distinctions A – D
Box 6 Distinctions E - Z

In addition there are five bound volumes containing around 450 photographs. Mr J.W. Lister, Hove's Chief Librarian, was responsible for collecting the information.

Books

Ainsworth Major J.F., *The Royal Sussex Regiment,* 1972
Allingham H., with Goodwin D., *Kitchener's Last Volunteer,* Edinburgh, 2008
Anderson J., editor, *World War I Witness Accounts,* Leicester, 2009
Blighty Brighton, Brighton 1991, QueenSpark Book 26
Carder T., & Harris R., *Albion A-Z,* Brighton, 1997
Carder T., & Harris R., *Seagulls,* Brighton, 1993
Chambers *Biographical Dictionary* 9th edition, London, 2011
Collins *Encyclopaedia of Military History* 4th edition, London, 2007
Corrigan G., *Sepoys in the Trenches,* Stroud, 2006
Doyle Sir Arthur Conan, *Memories and Adventures,* 1924 reprinted 1989
Gooch J., *A History of Brighton General Hospital,* London, 1980
Hayward J., *Myths and Legends of the First World War,* Stroud, 2002

Healey B., *Hard Times and Easy Terms,* Brighton, 1980, QueenSpark Book 9

Marr A., *The Making of Modern Britain,* London, 2009

Mason E., *A Working Man,* Brighton, ND, QueenSpark Book 36

Middleton J., *A History of Hove,* London, 1979

Middleton J., *Encyclopaedia of Hove and Portslade*, 15 volumes (2000-2002)

Middleton J., *Hove in Old Picture Postcards,* Zaltbommel, 1983

Morris C., *British Bus Systems*, *No. 6 Southdown,* Glossop, Derbyshire, 1985

Parker G., *The Tale of a Boy Soldier*, Brighton, ND, QueenSpark Book 40

Paul A., *Poverty – Hardship but Happiness,* Brighton, 1974, QueenSpark Book 1

Pegler M., *Attack on the Somme,* Barnsley, 2006

Roberts J., *British Bus and Trolley Systems: No. 4. Brighton & Hove,* Glossop, Derbyshire, 1984

Sandys C., *Churchill Wanted Dead or Alive,* London, 1999

Simkins P., Jukes G., Hickey M., *The First World War,* Oxford, new edition 2013

Skelton, T., & Gliddon G., *Lutyens and the Great War,* London, 2008

Spackman Colonel W. C., *Captured at Kut,* Barnsley, 2008

Sweetman J., *Cavalry of the Clouds,* Stroud, 2010

Time-Life *The British Empire.* Part-work in 7 volumes, 1973

Van der Vat D., *The Dardenelles Disaster,* London, 2009

Walbrook H. M., *Hove and the Great War,* Hove, 1920

Warner P., *The Zeebrugge Raid,* Barnsley, 2008

Webb T. M. A., & Bird D.L., *Shoreham Airport,* Sussex, Gillingham, 2nd edition 1999

Internet

http://anglicanhistory.org/oceania/baddeley/reynolds1960.html

http://anglicanhistory.org/oceania/baddeley/

http://www.auspostalhistory.com/articles/2086.shtm/

Christopher Coomber, compiler of Hove's Roll of Honour and Portslade's Roll of Honour websites:

http://www.roll-of-honour.com/Sussex/Hove.html

http://www.roll-of-honour.com/Sussex/Portslade.html

Examiner (1 January 1918) online from the National Library of Australia

Various articles on the internet including ones on the Kekewiches, the Powells, *Oh! What a Lovely War* and Princess Clémentine of Belgium.

Index